# THE MILES THAT MAKE YOU

## HOW TO MAKE LIFE AN EPIC JOURNEY

### ALEX BOYLAN

Copyright © 2025 by Alex Boylan
First Paperback and Hardback Edition

All rights reserved. No part of this publication may be reproduced, distributed, or transmitted in any form or by any means, including photocopying, recording, or other electronic or mechanical methods, without the prior written permission of the publisher, except in the case of brief quotations embodied in critical reviews and certain other noncommercial uses permitted by copyright law.

For permission requests, write to the publisher, addressed "Attention: Permissions Coordinator," at the address below.

Some names, businesses, places, events, locales, incidents, and identifying details inside this book have been changed to protect the privacy of individuals.

Published by Freiling Agency, LLC.

P.O. Box 1264
Warrenton, VA 20188

www.FreilingAgency.com

HB ISBN: 978-1-963701-79-1
PB ISBN: 978-1-963701-80-7
E-book ISBN: 978-1-963701-81-4

# DEDICATION

*To my incredible parents, Dr. Reverend William and Miriam Boylan.
You created a foundation far richer than any material luxury could provide.
Thank you for giving me, my brother Andrew, and my sisters Andrea
and Alexis, the framework of hard work, resilience, and faith
that continues to guide my life. I love you.*

# CONTENTS

Introduction ................................................................. vii
1  Backpacks and Basement Shopping ............................... 1
2  The Day Turkey Changed Everything ............................. 7
3  The Power of a Story ................................................. 13
4  In Brasília ................................................................. 19
5  From Snowstorms to Sunshine ..................................... 27
6  Munich Bound ........................................................... 35
7  Spy Games in Prague .................................................. 43
8  Graduation, and Afterwards ......................................... 51
9  Chasing Money, Finding Misery ................................... 59
10 A (Quick) Return to College ........................................ 67
11 An Island, a Backpack, and No Plan B .......................... 77
12 *The Amazing Race* ................................................... 85
13 From Sweeping Floors to Hosting Shows ...................... 97
14 "Could You Do It for Free?" ...................................... 111
15 159 Days *Around the World for Free* ....................... 123
16 A Network Deal ...................................................... 131
17 Career Shifts .......................................................... 141
18 Building *The College Tour* ..................................... 153
19 *The College-to-Career Playbook* .............................. 161
20 Fatherhood and Lessons Learned ............................... 167
21 A Letter to My Son .................................................. 173

> "The truth is, we're all born with different 'backpacks.'"

# INTRODUCTION

I can still feel the sting of the wind on my face as we raced through the streets of San Francisco, the finish line just seconds away. After traveling the world—dodging traffic in Thailand, navigating backroads in Namibia, and barreling through cities in Australia—it all came down to this. One final sprint. Me and my best friend Chris Luca, hearts pounding, minds racing faster than our feet.

*The Amazing Race* wasn't just a TV show. For me, it was the culmination of every risk I'd ever taken, every decision to bet on myself when there was no safety net. It was the moment everything changed—and the moment I realized the power of a great story. Not a scripted, polished, Instagram-filtered story. But a real one. Full of chaos, setbacks, twists, and growth.

And that story didn't start with a million dollars on the line. It began in a small town on the North Shore of Boston called Georgetown, Massachusetts, with a hand-me-down backpack, a pastor's salary, and a family that believed in hard work more than handouts. My journey has taken me from favelas in Brazil to software boardrooms in Germany, from tending bar in the Caribbean to building hit TV series out of thin air—and now to campuses across the country, helping students imagine a future they never thought possible.

This book is about that journey. Not just mine—but yours, too.

Because the truth is, we're all born with different "backpacks." Some of us come into this world with privilege, some with pain. Some with opportunities laid out in front of us, and others with obstacles that seem impossible to climb. But what I've learned over the years—and what I want to pass along to you—is that it's not about the weight of the backpack you start with. It's about what you *do* with it, how you carry it. Where you take it. Who you become along the way.

This book isn't about fame or reality TV. It's not about chasing likes or building a "brand." It's about saying yes to the uncomfortable. Taking the leap when you don't know what's on the other side. Embracing detours and disasters because they're usually the things that teach us the most. It's about getting out of your own way, trusting the journey, and finding your story—not the one someone else wrote for you, but the one you get to write yourself.

We're going to cover a lot of ground—my early life, the wild adventures, the crashes and rebounds, and the lessons I wish I'd known earlier. Along the way, I'll share the practical tools and mindset shifts that helped me go from broke and lost to building a career I love. I'll talk about what it means to connect with people, to build relationships that last, and how to use your story—not your résumé—to open doors that would otherwise stay shut.

But most of all, I want this book to leave you feeling like you can do it, too. Not because you have it all figured out, but because you're willing to take the first step.

I don't know where you are on your journey right now. Maybe you're in high school, college, or trying to figure out your next move after a significant career shift. Perhaps you're already living your dream—or maybe you're stuck in a cubicle watching the clock tick toward 5 p.m., wondering what happened to that spark you used to have.

Wherever you are, this book is for you.

So let's start at the beginning—Georgetown, Massachusetts, on the North Shore of Boston. My dad's church. Hand-me-downs. Calendars to sell. A plane ticket to Brazil.

And a belief that if you stay curious, work hard, and lean into the discomfort—you'll be amazed where life can take you.

"When you grow up having to work for everything you get, taking risks doesn't seem so scary."

# 1

# BACKPACKS AND BASEMENT SHOPPING

I can still remember the smell of the church basement—musty carpet, wood polish, and that peculiar scent of old hymnals. The First Independent Congregational Church in America—Byfield Parish Church—wasn't just where my father preached; it was where I found my first "new" clothes. Except they weren't new at all.

## Pastor's Salary Realities

"Alex, I think these might fit you," my mother would say, pulling pants or a shirt from the church's goodwill closet. We called it "shopping," but it was really where families from the congregation donated their kids' outgrown clothes. On a pastor's salary on the North Shore of Boston, hand-me-downs weren't just practical—they were necessary.

Don't get me wrong. I had an incredible childhood. Freedom to roam. Parents who loved me. But money? That was scarce. If I wanted a bike, I worked for that bike. If I needed new sneakers, I saved up. Nothing was handed to me, and looking back, that was one of the greatest gifts my parents ever gave me.

Here's the thing about life that I've come to understand: we're all born with different backpacks. Some people come into this world with backpacks so heavy they can barely stand—poverty, illness, unstable homes. Others are born with practically nothing on their backs at all—privilege, opportunities, safety nets. Most of us fall somewhere in between.

I had loving parents, a stable home, and enough food on the table. But I also had financial limitations that shaped me in ways I couldn't appreciate until much later. My backpack wasn't the heaviest, but it had enough weight to teach me about work, value, and resilience.

"It's not about what backpack you're born with," my father would often say in different words. "It's about how you carry it, where you take it, and who you become along the way."

While my friends were heading to Disney World or fancy summer camps, my exposure to the world came through a different channel: my father's connections with missionaries. When I was fourteen, my dad took a sabbatical. Instead of staying home or taking us to a resort, he and my mom packed up the family—all four kids—and flew us to Istanbul, Turkey, on a shoestring budget.

## First Glimpse of the World: A Family Sabbatical Adventure

We backpacked from Istanbul, Turkey, to Scotland, traveling through Greece, France, and other European countries along the way. This wasn't a tourist vacation with hotels and guided tours. We stayed with missionaries my father knew, helping them with their work—feeding the homeless, building community gardens, whatever was needed.

I can still remember landing in Istanbul in 1991. The minaret calls to prayer, the smell of spices in the markets, the way people moved through the streets with purpose and rhythm, so different from our quiet Boston suburb. It was like walking into a different universe, and my fourteen-year-old mind was blown wide open.

"Dad, why don't they just leave their shoes on when they go to church?" I remember asking on our second day.

He laughed. "Alex, this is their world. We're the foreigners here. We're the ones who do things differently."

That single insight—that I wasn't the center of the world, that my "normal" was someone else's "foreign"—shifted something fundamental in me. The world was vast, varied, and waiting to be explored. And I wanted more.

When you grow up in a small town with limited resources, your imagination becomes your greatest asset. I'd listen to my father's missionary friends tell stories about building schools in Kenya or medical clinics in

Peru, and I'd lie awake at night wondering what it would be like to stand in those places myself. So one night at dinner I announced to my parents, "I want to be a foreign exchange student."

My mother, ever the problem-solver, said, "I love the idea, but we need to figure out how to pay for this." That was a fair question. We didn't have money for fancy family vacations, let alone sending me to live abroad. But here's another lesson my parents instilled in me: if you want something badly enough, you find a way.

So at fifteen, when I found a foreign exchange program with a soccer connection in Brazil, my mother helped me develop a plan. I will share more with you about what happened in the next chapter. But, she bought over 2,000 advent calendars in bulk—religious calendars leading up to Christmas with important dates and reminders—and I had to sell every single one to pay her back and fund my exchange.

Door to door, business to business, I hustled those calendars. Each sale was another step toward Brazil. Each "no" (and there were plenty) just meant I needed to knock on another door. Looking back, I realize I wasn't just selling calendars—I was learning persistence, resilience, and the value of hard work—skills that would serve me far better than any amount of money my parents could have given me.

That's the beauty of being born with a particular kind of backpack. When you grow up without financial advantages, you develop other strengths: ingenuity, grit, and appreciation for what you earn. You learn to see opportunities where others see obstacles.

Growing up in Georgetown is where I found my first passion: soccer. It gave me discipline, teamwork, and an outlet for my competitive nature. But even as I was kicking balls on that field, my mind was often elsewhere—wondering what it would be like to play soccer in Brazil, to speak another language, to live in a place where everything was different.

The North Shore shaped me, but it never defined me. My father's church taught me values, my mother's resourcefulness taught me independence, and that first glimpse of the wider world during our family backpacking trip planted a seed of curiosity that would grow into something I never could have imagined.

Sometimes people ask me how I developed the courage to take the leaps I've taken throughout my life—to live in Brazil at sixteen, to move to the island of St. John with no plan, to travel the world with no money. The truth is, that courage was forged in the ordinary circumstances of my childhood. When you grow up having to work for everything you get, taking risks doesn't seem so scary. You already know you can survive on little, adapt to new circumstances, and build something from nothing.

Those early years taught me the most valuable lesson of all: get comfortable being uncomfortable because it's in those uncomfortable spaces—whether it's wearing someone else's hand-me-downs or navigating a foreign country—that you grow into the person you're meant to become.

> "Home isn't a place, it's where you find your purpose."

# 2

# THE DAY TURKEY CHANGED EVERYTHING

I stood in the Istanbul airport, clutching my worn backpack, jet-lagged and disoriented. The cacophony of announcements in Turkish, the unfamiliar alphabet on signs, the sea of faces that looked nothing like those back in Georgetown—it was overwhelming for a fourteen-year-old kid who'd never left the country.

## Fourteen and Far From Home

On our first taxi ride from the airport into the city, my father's missionary friend made the two taxis that were driving my family split into two cars pull over on the highway, arguing, as the local missionary was upset at getting ripped off. It felt like chaos.

"Dad, are you sure this is a good idea?" I whispered.

My father, the pastor of The Byfield Parish Church, smiled with the calm confidence that defined him. "Alex, we are fine, and this is going to change how you see the world."

He had no idea just how right he would be.

The year was 1991, and my father had earned a sabbatical after years of service to our church. Instead of using this time for rest or academic pursuits like most clergy might, he decided to take our entire family—all four of us kids—on what can only be described as a missionary backpacking adventure from Turkey to Scotland.

This wasn't the kind of trip most American families took in the early '90s. We weren't staying in hotels or following tourist routes. This was "Airbnbs before Airbnbs existed," as I like to say now. We were staying in the homes of missionaries my father knew through his church connections, sleeping in locals' houses, and immersing ourselves in their daily work and world.

Our first stop was Istanbul, where we stayed with our missionary friends running a church and community outreach program. I remember waking up in the middle of the night to the call to prayer echoing across the city, the sound both haunting and beautiful. The family's daughter, a bit younger than me, showed me how to wash my hands before meals in the traditional way and taught me basic Turkish phrases that I practiced with fierce determination.

"Teşekkür ederim," I repeated carefully, thanking our hosts for the breakfast of olives, white cheese, cherries, and cucumbers—so different from my usual cereal.

What struck me most wasn't just the different food or language, but how quickly what felt foreign began to feel familiar. After just a few days, I was navigating the local markets, bargaining for fruit (primarily through hand gestures), and playing soccer in a dusty lot with kids who couldn't speak a word of English but still became my friends for the day.

From Turkey, we traveled to Greece, where we stayed with another missionary family on the outskirts of Athens. I remember climbing the hill to the Parthenon, my history textbooks suddenly coming alive before my eyes. But the real education wasn't in the ancient ruins—it was in the everyday moments. Assisting the family in distributing food within a refugee community. Learning to ride the public bus system by trial and error, and figuring out how to communicate when words failed.

"Watch and learn," my mother advised when I felt frustrated by the language barrier. "Your eyes and ears will tell you more than your mouth ever could."

She was right. I began to notice how people greeted each other, how families interacted, and how communities functioned. I observed cultural norms and social expectations that no guidebook could explain. I was developing what I now recognize as cultural intelligence—the ability to adapt and function effectively in environments different from your own.

We continued our journey through Greece, France, and England, eventually making our way to Scotland. In each place, we didn't just visit—we lived, even if briefly. We shopped at local markets, cooked in missionary kitchens, and participated in their community work. One day we might be helping paint a community center; the next, we'd be distributing supplies to a homeless encampment, the next day, we would be visiting the Palace of Versailles.

I remember a particular evening in a small French Village outside of Paris. We were staying with an American family who had been working there for nearly a decade. After dinner, sitting in their modest courtyard under a canopy of grapevines, I asked the husband, "Don't you miss home?"

He looked at me thoughtfully. "Home isn't a place, Alex. It's where you find purpose."

That simple statement settled deep in my consciousness, though I wouldn't fully understand its impact until years later.

The trip wasn't without challenges. There were times we got lost, days when the language barrier felt insurmountable, moments when cultural differences led to misunderstandings. My siblings and I occasionally complained about missing American food, friends, or the comforts of home. But my parents never wavered. Complaining wasn't allowed in my family.

## Learning to Navigate Alone

One day, we were in Brussels. We had split up—my mom and sisters went into the city for some last-minute chocolate shopping, while my dad, brother, and I hauled all the luggage to the train station en route to the airport.

Our train arrived with little warning, and we had too many bags to carry on in one trip. It became a chaotic scramble: bags in, bags out, jumping on and off the train as the seconds ticked down. Just as I jumped off the train to grab the final bags, the doors slid shut behind me.

I turned around just in time to see my brother Andrew's arm shoot out the window, tossing my train ticket onto the platform. "Grab the next train!" he shouted.

And just like that, they were gone.

Now my dad had a choice: stay on the train with my sixteen-year-old brother and all our luggage, or get off and try to find his fourteen-year-old son—me—who was now alone in the Brussels train station.

Things spiraled fast. Someone told my father the train I might have gotten on was heading to Paris. That became his operating theory: his teenage son, accidentally bound for another country.

But I hadn't gone anywhere. I stayed put.

Somehow, amid the unfamiliar signs and the maze of platforms—there must have been a hundred of them, all labeled in Flemish or French—I remembered what we'd done on previous travel days. Head to the main terminal, check the departure board, and find the right platform. That's what I did. I was nervous, sure. But I also felt, oddly, like I had this.

Thirty minutes later, as I stood on the platform ready to board, I heard something unexpected over the intercom:

"Alex Boylan."

My name. Echoing through the station.

I grabbed the two bags I'd managed to hold onto and headed toward the main concourse. As I turned the corner, I saw my dad.

He fell to his knees.

Just dropped, overwhelmed, in the middle of the station. Not because I was lost, but because I'd been found. We hugged, and we laughed, and we took the right train to the airport, where we found my brother. Later that day, we reunited with my mom and sisters.

But I'll never forget the feeling of being alone in that vast station—and the pride, even at fourteen, of figuring it out myself. "Discomfort is the price of growth," as my mother would say. "Lean into it."

Those words became a mantra I've carried throughout my life. Get comfortable being uncomfortable. It's in those awkward spaces that we learn, adapt, and discover what we're capable of.

By the time we reached Scotland—our final destination before heading home—I was a different person than the kid who had left Georgetown, Massachusetts, weeks earlier. I had navigated foreign cities, crossed language barriers, adapted to other customs, and learned to find connection despite differences. I had discovered that I loved the feeling of stepping into the unknown and finding my footing.

## THE DAY TURKEY CHANGED EVERYTHING

On one of our last nights abroad, staying near a Scottish loch (another budget-friendly accommodation choice), I remember looking up at stars that somehow seemed both foreign and familiar.

"Dad," I said, "when can we do this again?"

He laughed. "Maybe the better question is: what will you do with what you've learned?"

That question has guided me ever since. The lessons from that backpacking trip have informed every major decision I've made—from becoming an exchange student in Brazil to racing around the world for a million dollars to traveling the globe with no money at all.

I learned that borders are human constructions and that people everywhere share fundamental desires for connection, purpose, and belonging. I discovered that adaptability is more valuable than comfort, and that the best education happens outside the classroom. I realized that my circumstances—growing up with limited financial resources—had prepared me well for navigating a world where creativity and resilience matter more than privilege.

Most importantly, I began to see myself as a citizen of the world rather than just a kid from the North Shore of Boston. That perspective shift opened doors I never knew existed and gave me the courage to walk through them.

When people ask me how I developed the confidence to take the risks I've taken throughout my life, I often point to that family backpacking trip. At fourteen, I discovered that the world was both vastly bigger and considerably smaller than I had imagined. Bigger in its endless variety of cultures, languages, and landscapes; smaller in how easily connections could form across those differences.

My father's sabbatical adventure didn't just change how I saw the world—it changed how I saw myself in it. It planted the seed of curiosity that would grow into a lifetime of exploration and a career built around sharing stories that connect us across our differences.

That backpack I clutched so nervously in the Istanbul airport? It became a symbol of possibility rather than a burden. And I've been packing it for new adventures ever since.

> "If you want something badly enough, you find a way."

# 3

# THE POWER OF A STORY

Home from our family backpacking adventure, I returned to the familiar routines of Georgetown High School—classes, soccer practice, hanging out with friends. But something had shifted inside me. The world beyond the North Shore now felt less like an abstract concept and more like a place I belonged.

**Stories That Spark Wanderlust**

One evening after our arrival back to the States my older sister's good friend Bob Curtis came over. He began reminiscing of his foreign exchange in New Zealand. Here I am fresh off a trip with the family to a foreign land hearing stories of this solo journey to a country I knew very little about. And that is what spurred me wanting to be a foreign exchange student as soon as possible.

As we passed dishes around our modest dining table, Bob began telling stories about his year abroad and living with a host family in Auckland. Learning to play rugby, struggling to understand local slang, and hiking through landscapes that looked like something from another planet.

I couldn't take my eyes off him. While the rest of the family continued eating, I sat there with my fork hovering midair, mesmerized.

"So there I was, trying to navigate this roundabout on the wrong side of the road," Bob laughed, recounting his first driving lesson. "My host dad was shouting, 'Left! Left!' and I kept turning right!"

It wasn't just the exotic locations or adventures that captivated me. It was how Bob had transformed. He seemed more sure of himself, more worldly, more complete somehow. He had stories that made everyone lean in and listen—stories that were uniquely his.

After dinner, while Andrea and Bob caught up in the living room, I peppered him with questions.

"How did you get to go? Did they speak English? What was the hardest part? Did you miss home?"

Bob answered patiently, explaining how he'd found a program called AFS (American Field Service) that arranged international student exchanges. "They have scholarships too," he added, knowing our family's financial situation without my having to mention it.

That night, lying in bed, I made a decision: I was going to be an exchange student—as soon as possible. My family backpacking trip had given me a taste of the wider world; now I wanted to dive in fully, to live in another culture rather than just passing through.

The next morning, I approached my mom. "I want to be an exchange student," I announced. "Like Bob."

To her credit, she didn't dismiss the idea outright, despite knowing the financial implications. Instead, she asked, "Where would you want to go?"

I hadn't thought that far ahead. My initial instinct was New Zealand, like Bob. But then I remembered the part of our conversation where he mentioned that AFS had programs all over the world, including places where I could play soccer.

Soccer had been my passion since I was old enough to kick a ball. On the field, I found focus, camaraderie, and a sense of accomplishment that school sometimes failed to provide. Although I wasn't the top student academically, I found my confidence on the soccer field.

"Somewhere I can play soccer," I replied. "Somewhere warm." Growing up with New England winters has given me an appreciation for sunshine that borders on reverence.

My mother, always practical but optimistic and supportive, nodded. "Let's look into it."

Over the next few weeks, we researched AFS programs together. The costs were daunting—several thousand dollars for a year abroad, plus airfare and other expenses. For a pastor's family on a tight budget, it might as well have been a million.

"Maybe when you're older," my father suggested gently, seeing the disappointment on my face.

But I wasn't willing to defer this dream. I kept thinking about what my mom often said during that backpacking trip: "Discomfort is the price of growth." I was ready to pay that price.

"What if I earn the money myself?" I proposed.

My parents exchanged glances—that look parents give each other when they're trying to decide if their child is being hopelessly naive or impressively determined.

"How would you do that?" my mother asked.

I didn't have a specific plan yet, but I knew I would find a way. My parents had always taught us that if we wanted something, we had to work for it. Whether it was a new bike or a pair of soccer cleats, I'd learned to save, to hustle, to find creative solutions.

"I'll figure it out," I insisted. "Just help me find the right program."

My mother, seeing my determination, made a decision that would change the course of my life. She contacted AFS and found a program in Campina Grande, Brazil, where I could attend high school and play soccer with a local team.

Brazil! The country of Pelé, of jogo bonito—"the beautiful game." The mere thought made my heart race. It was perfect.

But the cost remained a massive obstacle: thousands of dollars that my family simply didn't have. That's when my mother came up with an unusual solution.

## 2,000 Calendars

"I can buy these advent calendars in bulk," she explained, showing me a calendar that you would open up a piece for each day, where a Christian message and some chocolate were leading up to Christmas day. "You sell them at a markup, pay me back for the initial investment, and keep the profit for your exchange program."

She bought over 2,000 calendars—an amount that seemed impossible to sell. But she believed I could do it, and that belief was all I needed.

For months, I became a one-person advent calendar-selling machine. I went door to door to literally every house in Georgetown. I set up a table outside the local *Crosby's* grocery store on weekends. I convinced relatives to buy multiple calendars as gifts. I approached small offices and pitched them on buying calendars for their employees.

Every "no" was just a step toward the next potential "yes." Every dollar earned was another mile closer to Brazil. I kept a meticulous tally, watching the numbers grow painfully slowly at first, then with increasing momentum as I refined my sales pitch and expanded my territory to other towns beyond Georgetown.

My friends thought I was crazy. "You're spending your whole sophomore year selling calendars just to go to school in another country?" they'd ask. "Why not just stay here and hang out like normal?"

But normal wasn't what I was after. I'd gotten a glimpse of what lay beyond the familiar boundaries of Georgetown, and I couldn't unsee it. I wanted more—more experiences, more challenges, more opportunities to discover what I was capable of.

The calendar sales taught me persistence, resilience, and the power of incremental progress. Each small success built my confidence. Each setback forced me to get creative. By the end of that year, I had sold every single calendar and earned enough to fund my exchange experience.

The day I handed my mother a check to reimburse her for the initial investment was one of the proudest moments of my young life. I'd done it—I'd made the seemingly impossible possible through nothing but determination and hard work.

As I prepared for departure, packing that same backpack I'd carried through Turkey and Greece, I realized something important: the journey to Brazil had already changed me, even before I set foot on the plane. I'd learned that I could create opportunities rather than waiting for them to appear. I'd discovered that my financial limitations weren't walls but hurdles—challenging to overcome, but far from impossible.

Most importantly, I'd internalized a lesson that would guide me throughout life: if you want something badly enough, you find a way. Not an excuse, not a compromise—a way.

Standing at the airport, preparing to board the first of nine flights that would eventually take me to Campina Grande, I thought about Bob, whose stories had ignited this dream. Now I was writing my own story, one calendar sale at a time.

My mother hugged me goodbye, whispering, "Be safe, OK, Alex?" She made sure I had my $600 in twelve $50 traveler's checks (all the money I would have down in Brazil). Then she added with a smile, "Just promise me one thing—no more calendar sales when you get back."

I laughed, shouldered my backpack, and walked toward the gate. I looked back one last time and noticed my mother was crying. A few tears ran down my face, too. I wasn't sure why. I was pretty nervous—maybe even a little scared. But I knew my parents supported me. It was time to go.

Brazil awaited—and with it, the next chapter of a life shaped by saying yes to the uncomfortable, the challenging, and the unknown.

"The world is waiting, not just to be seen, but to be lived in."

# 4

# IN BRASÍLIA

Nine flights.

That's what it took to get from Boston to Campina Grande, Brazil, in 1994.

I first landed in Miami, FL, and then in Rio de Janeiro, a big city. Then I got on another plane that made stops all the way up the coast. Each connection took me further from everything familiar and closer to a world I could barely imagine. It all felt surreal. At each stop, I double-checked to make sure this wasn't where I was supposed to get off. I worried I might miss it! I listened intently for the words "Campina Grande" every time we landed. By the time I landed at my final destination—little more than a landing strip—exhaustion had morphed into a strange, electric anxiety.

I was sixteen years old, standing in a small regional airport in northeastern Brazil with a backpack, rudimentary Spanish that wouldn't help me with Portuguese, and the name of a host family I'd never met. I had never felt more alone—or more alive.

A middle-aged couple approached me, smiling tentatively. "Alex?" the man asked, pronouncing my name with an unfamiliar accent. I nodded, and they embraced me as if I were a long-lost relative. My host parents. They spoke no English. None at all. I realized that everyone else behind them—about 15 people, in total—were all here to see me. It was their friends and community, all here at the airport, who made sure I felt welcome.

### In a New World

That first car ride from the airport remains vivid in my memory. The windows were down because there was no air conditioning, warm tropical air rushing in, carrying unfamiliar scents—spices, diesel fuel, flowering trees I couldn't name. My host parents chatted animatedly in Portuguese while I nodded and smiled, understanding nothing except my name when it occasionally punctuated their conversation.

We pulled up to a modest home in a neighborhood that looked nothing like Georgetown, Massachusetts. Low concrete buildings painted in bright colors, metal gates, and tile roofs. Kids are playing soccer in the street with a makeshift ball. Motorbikes weaving through traffic. Everything was different. Everything.

"Sua casa," my host father said, gesturing toward the house. Your home.

The next morning, reality hit hard. I was enrolled in a local high school where every class was taught in Portuguese. I sat in the back of the classroom that first day, watching the teacher's lips move, catching maybe one word in fifty. Students stared, whispered, and pointed. I was the American—the gringo—and I was completely lost.

By lunchtime, I was ready to call my parents and beg to come home. Except calling the United States in 1994 meant going to a special international phone center, paying an exorbitant rate, and arranging a time in advance. This wasn't the era of cell phones and FaceTime. Communication home was limited to a monthly phone call and handwritten letters that took weeks to arrive.

I was truly on my own in a way that's hard to imagine in today's hyper-connected world.

After school, my host brother took me to soccer practice with the local team I'd be playing with. Soccer—futebol—was my lifeline. On the field, I didn't need to speak Portuguese. The language of the game was universal. Pass, shoot, defend. Within minutes, I went from being the weird American kid to a potential teammate.

"Bom, bom!" the coach shouted when I executed a clean pass. Good, good! I understood that much.

The walk to and from soccer practice became a daily education. I walked solo through areas that I later learned were favelas—informal settlements where the poorest residents lived in makeshift homes pieced together from whatever materials they could find. Children with no shoes played in dirt alleys. Women carried impossibly large bundles of laundry

## IN BRASÍLIA

on their heads. Old men sat in plastic chairs in front of small shops, watching the world pass by.

It was confronting and humbling. The poverty I witnessed was far beyond anything I'd seen, even growing up with limited means myself. I began to understand that my "hand-me-down clothes" childhood was still draped in privileges I'd taken for granted—clean water, reliable electricity, safe streets, access to education.

The public transportation system became my next challenge. To get to school, I needed to navigate a complex network of buses with no maps, no schedules, and no ability to ask for directions. My host family showed me once, and after that, I was expected to figure it out.

The first time I attempted it alone, I got hopelessly lost. I ended up in a neighborhood far from where I needed to be, with night falling and no way to call for help. A kind elderly woman saw my obvious confusion and, using gestures and simple words, repeated slowly, helped me find the right bus. That night, I wrote in my journal: "Today I was completely lost and survived. And I loved it."

Language came slowly, painfully. I carried a small notebook everywhere, writing down new words phonetically. I'd point at objects and repeat whatever my host family said. I watched Brazilian television with the concentration of a bomb defuser, trying to match words to actions. At night, I'd study by candlelight when the unreliable electricity went out.

After two months, I had my first dream in Portuguese. I woke up amazed, realizing that my brain was processing the language even while I slept. By three months, I could carry on basic conversations. By four, I was arguing with my host brother about which soccer team was superior and telling jokes that actually made people laugh.

The immersion was total, and the growth exponential. I was becoming someone new—someone who could navigate a foreign city, communicate in a language I hadn't known existed a year earlier, and built relationships across profound cultural differences.

Soccer became the center of my social life. I played with my school team, my neighborhood team, and anyone who gathered for an impromptu game in the streets. The Brazilian style of play was different—more creative, more expressive, less structured than what I'd known in the

U.S. I absorbed it all, adapting my own play and falling deeper in love with the beautiful game.

My teammates became my first real friends in Brazil. After games, we'd sit in outdoor cafés drinking guaraná (a sweet, caffeinated Brazilian soda) and eating pastéis (fried pastry pockets filled with meat or cheese). My Portuguese improved the most during these hangouts, where the conversation flowed as freely as the drinks.

"You speak like a baby," my friend Ricardo would tease, "but at least now we understand the baby."

School remained challenging, but as my language skills improved, so did my ability to participate. I'd never been a standout student back home, but the experience of learning in such adverse conditions taught me that I was capable of far more than I'd given myself credit for. I developed new study habits, new ways of concentrating, and new methods for absorbing information.

## From Gringo to Grateful Guest

I called my host parents "mãe" and "pai"—mom and dad. My host siblings felt like brothers and sisters. We shared meals, chores, celebrations, and occasional conflicts, just like a real family. They embraced me not as a visitor but as a new son, one who happened to have been born elsewhere. Yet even still, cultural and language differences made it difficult to connect very deeply with them. Home life was definitely a challenge. But I was treated like an adult, and I had all the freedom I wanted to venture out and grow.

The monthly phone calls home to Massachusetts became shorter as the year progressed. Not because I missed my family less, but because I had more to tell and less time to tell it in. How could I possibly compress the daily miracle of my new life into a fifteen-minute international call?

Instead, I wrote long letters, filling pages with descriptions of Brazilian food, the music that played constantly in the streets, the religious festivals that shut down the entire city, the soccer matches where passion bordered on religion. I wanted my family to see Brazil through my eyes, to understand how this place was changing me.

One night, about four months into my stay, I was helping my host mother prepare dinner. She asked about my family back home, and I showed her a photo of my parents standing in front of our church in Georgetown.

"Seu pai é pastor?" she asked, pointing to my father, who was wearing a robe that he sometimes wore when he preached to the congregation. "Is your father a pastor?"

I nodded, and she smiled with new understanding. "Então nós somos irmãos." Then we are brothers and sisters.

She explained that although we came from different countries, spoke different languages, and had different customs, we shared something fundamental—faith. The connection transcended our surface differences. It was a moment of profound recognition, one that shaped my understanding of how people connect across apparently vast divides.

As my exchange year neared its end, I realized something important: this experience had given me my first real story. Not just an anecdote or a tale of a minor adventure, but a genuine story of transformation. I had arrived, barely able to ask for water; I was leaving almost fluent in a new language. I had arrived dependent and fearful; I was leaving independent and confident.

When I returned home, I found that people leaned in when I talked about Brazil. Teachers, friends, neighbors—they'd listen with genuine interest as I described walking through favelas to soccer practice, navigating the chaotic public transportation system, or the festivals that filled Campina Grande's streets with music and dancing.

I hadn't planned it, but I'd created something valuable: a perspective that was uniquely mine, formed by immersion in a world most people in Georgetown would never see. I had differentiated myself not through exceptional academic achievement or athletic prowess, but through the simple choice to step far outside my comfort zone.

Brazil gave me more than memories; it gave me confidence that would color every future decision. If I could thrive there, at sixteen, speaking no Portuguese when I arrived, what else might I be capable of? The question itself was liberating.

Years later, when faced with risky decisions or uncertain paths, I would think back to that terrified sixteen-year-old standing in a small

Brazilian airport, utterly alone and completely alive. And I would remind myself: you've done harder things than this. You'll find a way.

Brazil wasn't just my first big adventure—it was the template for every adventure that followed. It taught me that the most worthwhile experiences often begin with feeling utterly lost, that genuine connection can happen across the most apparent barriers, and that our capacity to adapt and grow is far greater than we imagine.

Most importantly, it confirmed what that family backpacking trip had first suggested: the world was waiting, not just to be seen, but to be lived in. And I was just getting started.

"Learn to thrive at the edge of your comfort zone."

# 5

# FROM SNOWSTORMS TO SUNSHINE

When I returned to Georgetown High School for my senior year, everything felt different. My classmates were exactly the same, but I had been fundamentally changed by my year in Brazil. I'd walked through favelas, learned a new language, navigated public transportation in a foreign city, and played soccer in a country where it was practically a religion. How could I go back to worrying about prom dates and cafeteria drama?

**Senior Year Disconnect**

The truth is, I couldn't—not completely. Brazil had expanded my worldview and given me a taste of something I couldn't forget. As senior year progressed and college applications loomed, I found myself thinking less about following the typical path and more about creating my own.

"So, have you decided where you're applying?" my guidance counselor asked during one of our college planning sessions.

I had a clear answer, but it wasn't what she expected. "Somewhere warm with a Division I soccer program and international business."

She blinked, clearly hoping for specific school names. "That's... broad. What about schools in the Northeast? Your grades might not be great, but with soccer coaches recruiting you, and with your extracurriculars, you've got a shot at some decent schools."

"No more New England winters," I interrupted, perhaps a bit too firmly. "I spent nearly a year near the equator. I'm done with snow."

She sighed and pulled out a different set of college brochures. This was the mid-90s—we didn't have the internet to research schools or virtual tours to explore campuses. It was viewbooks, brochures, and maybe a campus visit if you could afford it.

My parents were supportive but realistic. "We can help some," my mother said, "but you'll need scholarships or loans for most of it." As a pastor's kid, I'd always understood the financial limitations. College would be largely on my own dime, which made the decision even more consequential (although I didn't really know much about money then).

Soccer became my ticket. I was a naturally gifted player, and spending some time in Brazil had elevated my game. I played with a different style now—more fluid, more creative, more intuitive. College recruiters noticed. But because I was from a small town and small high school, going to a Division I program was a stretch. I'm grateful my parents instilled confidence in me to aim high, because lots of Division II and III recruiters told me I couldn't play Division I because of the small high school league—The Cape Ann League—I played in throughout high school. But I had some experience with the Olympic Development team and a club team called Mosaic United, and I felt confident I could play at the Division I level.

Several schools expressed interest, but one school stood out.

## Jacksonville University: The Perfect Fit

Located in Florida, Jacksonville University checked my "warm weather" box emphatically. It had a respectable Division I soccer program where I could potentially contribute immediately (though the coach made it clear that there were no guarantees anyone would make the team, so I was nervous going down to training camp). And importantly, it offered an international business (rare, at that time) program that would prepare me for the global career I was beginning to envision.

The campus visit sealed the deal. Walking around in shorts in February—girls in bikinis and the beach just 20 minutes from campus—while my friends back home were shoveling snow felt like a victory in itself. The palm trees, the river running alongside campus, the view of downtown Jacksonville across the river from campus, the diverse student body—it all felt right. Different enough from Georgetown, Massachussets to be exciting, but familiar enough to be manageable.

"This is it," I told my parents on the phone that evening. "This is where I'm going."

There was another factor in my decision, though I didn't fully articulate it at the time: Jacksonville was just unfamiliar enough to maintain that edge of discomfort I'd grown to value. It wasn't Brazil, but it wasn't the North Shore of Boston either. It was a new environment that would require adaptation, new relationships, and new systems to navigate.

I'd discovered something important about myself during that time abroad: I thrived at the edges of my comfort zone. Too much comfort made me restless; too much discomfort was overwhelming. But that sweet spot in between—where I was stretched but not broken—that's where growth happened. Jacksonville felt like it would provide exactly that.

Arriving on campus as a freshman was both exciting and sobering. Exciting because it represented a new chapter, a step toward that international career I'd begun to imagine. Sobering because, despite scholarships and financial aid, I was taking on a bit of debt for this opportunity.

I couldn't know the answer then, but I committed anyway, believing that education—especially education that expanded my worldview—was an investment worth making. Whatever it cost in dollars, the experience would pay dividends in opportunity and perspective.

College life suited me. The classes in my international business major fascinated me—economics, marketing, management, all with a global focus. I soaked up theories about cross-cultural business practices, international trade, and global markets. After Brazil, these weren't abstract concepts but frameworks that helped me understand experiences I'd already had.

"In collectivist cultures like Brazil," a professor would explain, and I'd nod, recalling countless examples from my host family's prioritization of group harmony over individual achievement. When we discussed currency fluctuations, I remembered how the changing exchange rate had affected my monthly allowance during my exchange year. When I lived in Brazil, the country was under the short-lived currency "cruzeiro," which lost almost 50% of its value each month! I learned a lot about finance and currency debasement during that time—my $50 travelers' checks would be worth half that amount by the end of the month when cashed. So you had to think about it before making the move from dollars to cruzeiros.

Soccer provided structure and community. Practice schedules, road games, team responsibilities—they created the framework around which I built my academic and social life. The sport that had been my universal language in Brazil became my anchor at Jacksonville University.

But what I found most valuable about college wasn't in the curriculum or on the soccer field. It was the diverse community I found myself in. Jacksonville attracted students from across the U.S. and around the world. My roommate was from La Porte, Texas (which felt like another country back then). My soccer teammates came from England, Norway, Ghana, and Serbia.

Late-night conversations in dorm rooms and over cheap pizza introduced me to perspectives I'd never considered. A teammate from Norway helped me understand how Americans were perceived in Europe. A classmate from Japan explained concepts of face and honor that transformed how I thought about business relationships. Another teammate from Ghana gave me insights into systemic inequality that made me reconsider my own society.

I was building on what Brazil had started—developing a global mindset not just through textbooks but through relationships with people whose life experiences differed dramatically from my own.

My professors noticed this curiosity. Dr. Thompson, who taught International Marketing, pulled me aside after class one day during sophomore year.

"You ask different questions than the other students," he observed. "They want to know what's on the test. You want to know how things actually work in different contexts."

I explained about Brazil, about my family's trip backpacking Europe, and about selling calendars to fund my exchange year.

He nodded thoughtfully. "That explains it. You're not just studying international business; you've lived a version of it. You understand intuitively what others are trying to learn conceptually."

His observation stayed with me. The experiences I'd accumulated—not through privilege but through determination and hard work—were becoming assets. My story was becoming valuable.

College wasn't all smooth sailing. Financial pressures were always lurking around. Unlike many of my classmates, I couldn't call home for extra money when things got tight—at least, not too often (my parents did help when they could). I worked part-time jobs during the soccer off-season—in a local sports bar, refereeing intramural games—anything to keep the bills paid and reduce how much I needed to borrow. A couple summers I lifeguarded on Crane's Beach in Ipswich, Massachusetts, and bartended at the North Shore Music Theater in Beverly. When I started staying in Jacksonville year-round (to train with my teammates during the summer), I worked serving tables at Chili's off Atlantic Boulevard. Except during the soccer season, I always had a job.

Those jobs taught me as much as my classes did. Working in the service industry, in particular, developed skills no business course could teach: how to read people, how to de-escalate tense situations, how to make customers feel valued, how to manage multiple priorities under pressure. Years later, these would prove just as valuable as the theories and frameworks from my formal education.

As junior year approached, I found myself at another decision point. The international business program recommended an internship, preferably in a region relevant to one's career interests. Given my earlier experience in Brazil, Latin America seemed the obvious choice.

But something Dr. Thompson said gave me pause: "Don't just go where you're comfortable. Go where you'll be challenged in new ways."

Brazil had been a life-changing immersion, but I'd already experienced Latin American culture. Perhaps it was time to push beyond that familiarity into something completely different.

But before I tell you where I ended up, let me say this: that decision to prioritize warm weather and international business when choosing Jacksonville University might have seemed superficial or arbitrary to my high school guidance counselor, parents, and friends. In retrospect, though, it was one of the most important decisions I ever made.

Not because Jacksonville was objectively the "best" school, but because it was the right environment for me to continue growing in the direction I'd begun in Brazil. It provided just enough comfort to be functional and just enough challenge to keep me evolving.

The lesson? Sometimes the most important factor in a decision isn't prestige or conventional wisdom, but whether it allows you to keep moving forward on the path that feels authentically yours. For me, that path involved sunshine, soccer, and a curriculum that kept my eyes focused beyond American borders.

I couldn't have known then how perfectly this foundation would prepare me for what came next—an opportunity that would arrive unexpectedly, as the best opportunities often do, through a connection I never saw coming.

"Every mistake is a learning opportunity."

# 6

# MUNICH BOUND

Life's biggest opportunities often arrive when you least expect them, dressed as ordinary moments. For me, that moment came during a sweltering August afternoon in Georgetown, Massachusetts, while floating in a childhood friend's backyard pool.

## A Pool Conversation Changes Everything

I was home for summer break after my sophomore year at Jacksonville University. The Florida heat had followed me north, and I was killing time at my buddy Andrew Savelyev's house, waiting for him to return from an errand. His father, Mike, arrived home from work before Andrew did.

Mike was different from most parents in our blue-collar town. While most of our fathers worked in trades or local businesses, Mike was a genuine corporate guy—a sales executive for a European software company. He wore suits, traveled internationally, and spoke the language of global business that I was studying in college.

"Alex! What are you doing here?" he called out, spotting me in the pool.

I pulled myself out, dripping, and shook his hand. "Just waiting for Andrew. He should be back soon."

"How's school going? Jacksonville, right?" He loosened his tie as we talked.

"Yeah, it's great. Studying international business."

Mike's eyebrows raised with interest. "International business? What made you choose that?"

I reminded him about Brazil, about my growing fascination with global markets, about my dreams of a career that would let me work across cultures and borders.

He listened intently, nodding occasionally. As I was preparing to leave, Andrew still hadn't returned. Mike made an offhand comment that would change everything: "You know, Alex, you need work experience. College is great, but there is nothing better than doing the work."

I laughed it off. "Yeah, well, college is expensive enough already. Just trying to finish my degree without too much debt in four years." For some reason, graduating in four years was important to me.

But Mike persisted. "No, seriously. Book learning only gets you so far in international business. You need real experience in a foreign corporate environment."

As I headed for the door, he called after me: "If you want an internship with my company in Europe, let me know. I could set something up."

The entire drive back to Jacksonville (I usually drove 20 hours straight) for my junior year, those words echoed in my mind. An internship in Europe? With a legitimate international software company? It sounded incredible—and incredibly intimidating.

I'd done the study abroad thing already with Brazil. I knew what it meant to live in another culture. But this would be different. This wouldn't be living with a host family as a high school student. This would be navigating a professional environment in a foreign country, representing not just myself but an actual corporation.

The sensible part of me said to focus on finishing my degree efficiently. Take the required courses, graduate on time, and minimize debt. An internship would delay graduation and potentially cost more money than I have.

But another voice—the one that had pushed me to sell 2,000 calendars for my Brazil exchange, the one that thrived at the edge of my comfort zone—kept asking: When opportunity knocks this loudly, are you really going to pretend you're not home?

A week into the fall semester, I called Mike.

"I've been thinking about what you said," I told him. "About the internship."

"And?" I could hear the smile in his voice.

"If you're serious about it, I'd like to make it happen."

Mike didn't hesitate. "Great! I'll send you some information on our different European offices. Munich, Germany, Amsterdam, Netherlands, or Milan, Italy—you have some options. Think about where you'd like to go, and we'll start the paperwork."

The next few months were a blur of logistics. Working with my academic advisors to ensure the internship would count for credit. Figuring out the visa process. Finding affordable housing options. Deferring some of my scholarships.

I chose Germany—Munich—for practical and personal reasons. The office was doing innovative work in software that aligned with my interests. Germany's central location in Europe would make weekend travel more feasible. And something about the German reputation for precision and efficiency intrigued me. After the warmth and spontaneity of Brazilian culture, I was curious to experience something that seemed so different. I chose Munich—the company's international headquarters. My dad happened to speak some German from his time in the military, so I knew a little bit of the language. And you had to take a minor in a language in International Business, and I chose German because of my dad's experience with the language. I can remember being a kid and him teaching me little German words. I thought it was so cool!

## To Germany

In January 1998, I found myself stepping off a plane at Munich International Airport, carrying that same trusty backpack that had accompanied me to Brazil. But this time, I also carried a small suitcase of business clothes—my first real suit and a handful of ties my father had given me.

The deal was simple: three weeks of corporate lodging, a modest stipend, and then I was on my own dime, as it was a paid internship. Easy. Except for my first night, I answered the hotel room phone to a gravelly South African voice.

"Alex, right? I'm Tim—one of Mike's Executives. Meet me in the lobby. Thirty minutes."

Tim was mid-fifties, still rugby-broad in the shoulders, rumor had it he closed million-mark deals before breakfast. That night, he marched me through Munich's beer halls, teaching me to toast in Bavarian dialect and making sure the Maßkrüge never ran dry. Hours later, I looked up from my last stein and Tim was gone—vanished. No address, no goodnight, nothing. I zig-zagged across Munich's cobblestone streets, more fluent in panic than German, and somehow found my hotel before sunrise.

At eight sharp, the phone rang.

"Alex, you passed my first test, mate," Tim laughed. "Get yourself drunk in a foreign city and see if you can find your way home."

That first morning, standing in the lobby of a gleaming office building in my slightly-too-big suit, I felt like an impostor. What did I, a kid from the North Shore of Boston with zero corporate experience, have to offer a sophisticated European software company?

Sabine, the office manager, greeted me with efficient German courtesy. "Herr Boylan, willkommen. Folgen Sie mir bitte." Welcome, Mr. Boylan. Please follow me.

I smiled nervously, following her through a maze of cubicles to a decent-sized office. I actually had my own office in Munich (I'd mistakenly come to believe that this was normal for young, entry-level employees).

"Herr Schmidt, der amerikanische Praktikant ist hier." Mr. Schmidt, the American intern, is here.

Werner Schmidt looked up, assessing me with sharp blue eyes behind wire-rimmed glasses. Then he broke into a warm smile that transformed his severe appearance.

"Alex! Wonderful to meet you. Mike has told me good things." His English was precise but heavily accented. "Please, sit. We will discuss your project." A few days after I got settled, Mike flew in and explained the project and internship in more detail. I reported to three people—Mike Savelyev (the big boss), Tim Sowell (who had gotten me drunk and stranded on my first night), and Rob Stew (a more proper Englishman), two of Mike's chief executives.

That first meeting set the tone for my entire internship. Mike and his executive team were demanding but fair, expecting excellence but providing the guidance needed to achieve it. My assignment was both technical and strategic: to evaluate a new cloud-based contact management system the company was considering implementing across its European offices. Yes, it was the early stages of what we now know as CRM—Customer Relationship Management software.

Remember, this was 1998. Cloud computing wasn't yet mainstream. The idea of a database that multiple users could access remotely, updating in real-time, was still novel and somewhat revolutionary, especially for a sales force spread across different countries.

My task was to learn the system inside and out, test its capabilities, and make recommendations for implementation. It was a perfect project for an intern: contained enough to be manageable but significant enough to have a real business impact.

The technical aspects were challenging. I never took any computer science courses, so this was all foreign to me. I spent long hours in the office, experimenting with the system, documenting its features, and testing different scenarios. I really loved the challenge of cracking this thing.

But the greater challenge was cultural. The German corporate environment operated with unspoken rules and expectations that were very different from the American businesses I'd studied or the Brazilian contexts I'd experienced.

Meetings started precisely on time—not a minute late. Email communications were formal and structured. The hierarchy was clear and respected. Personal relationships developed slowly, built on demonstrated competence rather than immediate friendliness.

I made plenty of mistakes in those early weeks. I'd arrive at meetings with a casual "Hey, how's it going?" rather than the expected formal greeting. I'd send emails missing the proper salutations. I'd misinterpret the direct German communication style as rudeness rather than efficiency.

Each mistake became a learning opportunity. I observed carefully, adjusted my approach, and gradually began to navigate the environment more effectively. I'd done this before in Brazil—adapted to local norms and expectations—but the corporate context added new layers of complexity.

By the end of my first month, I had completed my initial analysis of the contact management system and prepared a presentation for Mike and his team. I'd worked through the weekend, refining my slides, practicing my delivery, and anticipating questions.

The morning of the presentation, I arrived early to set up the conference room. My hands shook slightly as I connected my laptop to the projector. This wasn't a college assignment; this was a professional deliverable for people whose actual jobs would be affected by my recommendations.

Mike arrived first, followed by Tim and Rob, who would all be impacted by the new system. I took a deep breath and began.

For the next thirty minutes, I walked them through my findings—the system's capabilities, its limitations, the implementation challenges, and my recommendations for customization and training. I'd prepared thoroughly, and it showed. The questions were specific and technical, but I was ready for them.

When I finished, Mike nodded approvingly. "This is great. But what are we going to do now that you've finished? You have many months left in your internship."

The sense of accomplishment was immediate and profound. I had delivered something of actual value to this company. My analysis would influence real business decisions. For the first time, I felt like a professional rather than a student playing at being one.

What happened next, though, took my internship in an unexpected direction—one that would teach me more about the reality of international business than any academic program ever could.

Later that afternoon, Mike called me into his office. "Alex, I have a proposition for you. Next week, I'm going up with some executives to Prague to meet with our Eastern European sales office. I think you should come with us. You can be our assistant and take notes."

I tried to hide my surprise. "Me? But I've only been here a month..."

Mike smiled. "Sometimes fresh eyes see what experienced ones miss. Pack your bag. The train leaves Monday morning."

That trip to Prague would be the first of many unexpected journeys during my internship—and the beginning of an education in the human side of international business that no textbook could provide. An education that would transform not just my understanding of business, but my understanding of my own potential and the unexpected paths a career can take when you say yes to opportunities that seem just beyond your reach.

"Winning in business means making life better for everyone."

# 7

# SPY GAMES IN PRAGUE

The train from Munich to Prague cut through the German countryside, then the Czech Republic, landscapes transforming outside the window as borders were crossed. I sat with three sales executives, all at least a couple of decades older than me, all with years of experience in international software engineering and sales. And then there was I, the American in the middle of his junior year of college, invited to this high-level meeting for reasons that still weren't entirely clear.

## From Intern to Intelligence Gatherer

"First time to Prague?" asked Tim Sowell, Mike's Chief Executive, with a perpetual five o'clock shadow.

"First time anywhere in Eastern Europe," I admitted.

He smiled. "You're in for a treat. Prague is magical—like stepping back in time."

I nodded, trying to look professional while secretly thrilled at the adventure. Just months earlier, I'd been sitting in lecture halls at Jacksonville University. Now I was crossing Europe on a business trip, part of a corporate team. The contrast was surreal.

We arrived in Prague late that afternoon. The sales team had meetings scheduled first thing the next morning, so we checked into our hotel—a nicer hotel than I had ever stayed in. We were staying at the Savoy—very high-end!

That evening was my first glimpse of the reality beneath the polished surface of international business. Over plates of goulash and Czech beer, the conversation shifted from pleasantries to candid shop talk. As the youngest person at the table, I was largely ignored, which turned out to be an unexpected advantage.

"The Hungarian office is still refusing to share their client data," Thomas complained to his colleagues, assuming I was too junior to pay attention. "How are we supposed to coordinate regional strategies when Miklos guards his contacts like state secrets?"

Another sales executive, Dieter, rolled his eyes. "It's not just Hungary. Romania is operating like its own fiefdom. Did you see last quarter's numbers? They're clearly cherry-picking deals and not recording the smaller ones in the system."

I listened quietly, absorbing everything. These weren't the kinds of issues discussed in formal meetings or documented in company reports. This was the real terrain of international business—the human frictions, the cultural tensions, the unwritten rivalries between offices and individuals.

The next day's meetings were cordial and productive on the surface. The Prague team presented their quarterly results, our Munich team shared new product roadmaps, and strategic goals were aligned—at least officially. But I noticed the undercurrents now: the careful phrasing that masked disagreements, the territorial body language when certain markets were discussed, the way information was selectively shared.

That evening, the senior executives retired early, leaving me with the younger sales reps from all offices across Europe. Free from the scrutiny of their bosses, these twenty-somethings were even more candid. Over rounds of Pilsner at a local pub, they vented frustrations that went far beyond what I'd heard the night before.

"The commission structure is broken," confided a Czech rep named Jakub. "They expect us to push the new enterprise software, but the compensation plan incentivizes the legacy products. It makes no sense."

A Frankfurt rep named Martina nodded emphatically. "And the training! How can they expect us to sell cloud solutions to enterprise clients when the last technical training we had was eighteen months ago?"

The conversation continued well into the night, covering everything from interdepartmental rivalries to specific executives who were blocking progress to market-specific challenges that headquarters failed to understand. I asked occasional questions, genuinely curious about their perspectives, and they opened up more and more. I wasn't trying to gather intelligence—I was just fascinated by the human dynamics of this international corporation, all while trying to pretend like I was a professional.

## The Power of Fresh Eyes

When we returned to Munich, I wrote up my analysis of the contact management system as Mike had requested. But during our one-on-one meeting, after we'd discussed the technical aspects, I hesitated.

"Is there something else, Alex?" Mike asked, noticing my reluctance.

"Well..." I chose my words carefully. "During the Prague trip, I heard some concerns from the sales teams. Things that might affect the implementation of this system and what you are trying to do strategically with your growth plan."

Mike leaned forward. "What kind of concerns?"

I shared what I'd learned—not as gossip, but as relevant context for the technology rollout we were planning. The tensions between offices. The misaligned incentives. The outdated training. The information silos.

I expected Mike to dismiss these as typical sales team complaints. Instead, he listened with intense focus, occasionally jotting notes. When I finished, he sat back in his chair and looked at me with new appreciation.

"Alex," he said finally, "do you understand what you've just shared with me?"

I shook my head, suddenly worried I'd overstepped.

"This information—about how the different national offices are actually functioning rather than how they report they're functioning—would never reach my level through normal channels. Ever." He tapped his pen on his notepad. "These are exactly the kinds of insights that can make or break a major technology implementation. And, frankly, they're the kinds of insights that can make or break a company's European strategy."

He studied me for a moment, then made a decision. "I'm changing your assignment. You'll continue with the implementation of the software, but I also want you to travel with me, Tim, and Rob to different offices. Observe, listen, and build relationships—especially with the younger staff. Then report back to me what you learn."

"Am I a spy?" I asked, with a fun smirk on my face.

Mike shook his head firmly. "Not a spy. Listen. There's a difference. You're not deceiving anyone or betraying confidences. You're simply paying attention to what people are actually saying rather than what they think I want to hear." He smiled. "And for whatever reason, people seem to talk openly around you."

That conversation marked the beginning of an unexpected evolution in my internship. Over the next several months, I traveled extensively with Mike and his executive team to Amsterdam, Belgium, and Italy. I sat in on strategy meetings, joined client presentations, and most valuably, participated in the informal conversations that happened in hotel bars, taxis, and coffee breaks.

At nineteen, I had no business being in most of these settings. I had zero technical knowledge and limited sales experience (aside from selling Advent calendars). But I had something that turned out to be unexpectedly valuable: I was a neutral party with no territorial agenda, no commission at stake, and apparently an approachable demeanor that encouraged candor.

People talked to me. The Hungarian sales director explained his reluctance to share client data, citing previous instances where German colleagues had poached his accounts. A French developer detailed technical problems with the new software that management had downplayed. An Italian office manager outlined the bureaucratic obstacles that delayed implementations in Southern European markets.

After each trip, Mike and I would debrief. I'd share what I'd learned, and he would ask insightful questions that helped me organize my observations. I wasn't just reporting facts; I was developing an analysis of the company's human dynamics. What motivated different teams? Where were the friction points? How did cultural differences manifest in business practices?

"You have a gift for this," Mike told me after a particularly illuminating debriefing about the Milan office. "You see patterns that most people miss."

The irony wasn't lost on me. As an international business student, I'd imagined my future in terms of market analysis, financial strategies, and global operations. I never anticipated that my most valuable skill would be simply listening to people and connecting the dots between their different perspectives.

The lifestyle that came with this new role was surreal for a kid from Georgetown, Massachusetts. Suddenly, I was staying in five-star hotels, dining in excellent restaurants, and traveling first-class across Europe—all on the company card. When Mike traveled, his accommodations were luxurious, and as his de facto assistant, I benefited from the same arrangements.

One evening, sitting on the terrace of a boutique hotel in Austria with Mike after a successful day of client meetings, I couldn't help but laugh at the improbability of my situation.

"What's amusing you?" he asked.

"Just thinking about the contrast," I explained. "A few months ago, I was eating ramen noodles in my dorm room to save money for textbooks. Now I'm drinking fine wine on a rooftop terrace overlooking the Alps."

Mike nodded thoughtfully. "Enjoy it, but don't be fooled by it."

"What do you mean?"

"This—" he gestured at our surroundings, "—is not what business is actually about. The nice hotels, expense accounts, business class flights... they're perks, not purposes. The real work happens in understanding human systems, solving problems, and creating value." He swirled his wine. "You're good at the real work, Alex. Don't get distracted by the trappings."

It was solid advice, but hard to fully absorb when you're nineteen and suddenly thrust into a world of corporate privilege. I won't lie—I enjoyed the lifestyle. Who wouldn't? But I also recognized its distorting effect. It would have been easy to believe that this was what a business career was about: nice suits, luxury hotels, expense account meals.

But in reality, it's so much more than that. Watching Mike carry the burden and stress of hundreds of people inspired me. It wasn't easy! But he truly cared about people—I never doubted. With as much as was on his plate every day, he never lost sight of what was most important. Winning in business meant making life better for everyone—employees, customers, and all of their families. That's what the boardroom is really about, and I'll never forget how much Mike's example taught me about that.

"So," Mike asked during a dinner in Munich toward the end of my internship, "are you ready to finish school and join the corporate world for real?"

I nodded enthusiastically. "Absolutely. This experience has been incredible."

He raised his glass. "To your future career, then. May it be as successful as it's started."

I returned to Jacksonville University with a transformed perspective. The internship had given me exactly what Mike had promised that day by his pool: real experience in international business. I'd seen firsthand how global companies actually functioned—not just the organizational charts and strategic plans, but the messy human realities underneath.

I'd also developed a skewed expectation of what corporate life would be like. In my mind, business meant important meetings in European capitals, strategic discussions over excellent meals, and the kind of life I'd glimpsed during those months in Germany.

That expectation would lead me to make choices after graduation that seemed logical at the time but ultimately placed me on a path toward profound dissatisfaction. But I'm getting ahead of myself.

What matters about the German experience isn't just what I learned, but how it continued to shape my approach to opportunities. Once again, I'd said yes to something that seemed slightly beyond my capabilities, stepped into uncomfortable territory, and discovered new aspects of myself in the process.

The "intern spy" role taught me that my value didn't always come from what I knew, but often from what I noticed—patterns, connections, human dynamics that others overlooked. It reinforced my growing conviction that the most interesting opportunities are rarely found within the parameters of standard job descriptions.

Most importantly, it confirmed that my "different backpack"—the one shaped by selling advent calendars and navigating Brazilian favelas—gave me perspectives and adaptability that couldn't be learned in classrooms. What I had initially seen as limitations were increasingly revealing themselves as unique advantages.

I didn't know it then, but this lesson would become crucial when my carefully constructed corporate career plans began to unravel, forcing me to reconsider what success really meant and how I wanted to pursue it.

> "Your credentials may get you considered, but your story is what gets you remembered."

# 8

# GRADUATION, AND AFTERWARDS...

When I returned to Jacksonville University for my senior year in 1998, I was a different person than the kid who'd left for Germany. I'd traded my college backpack for a briefcase (well, a laptop bag that I thought looked professional). I'd learned to order wine without looking clueless. I'd sat in boardrooms where decisions affecting thousands of employees were made. I was still a college student, but in my mind, I'd already joined the ranks of international business professionals.

Reality check: I was still the same kid from Georgetown, Massachusetts, with below-average grades who'd happen to have a couple of extraordinary experiences.

My final year flew by in a blur of capstone projects, soccer matches, and senior activities. We made the Sweet 16 that year in soccer (knocking off Duke, a perennial powerhouse along the way)—a big highlight for my soccer career. While my classmates stressed about finding their first "real" jobs, I felt oddly confident. After Germany, the corporate world didn't seem mysterious or intimidating—it felt like somewhere I'd already been.

This confidence wasn't entirely misplaced, but it was definitely incomplete. I understood certain aspects of international business in a way few new graduates could, but I had massive blind spots about what a typical corporate career actually entailed day-to-day. Those blind spots would come back to bite me later, but during senior year, my experiences gave me a genuine edge in one crucial area: job interviews.

### Interview Success: When Stories Trump GPAs

As graduation approached, I began applying for entry-level positions at international companies. My grades weren't spectacular—solid B's with a few A's in courses I was passionate about, and a couple of C's in subjects that failed to grab my interest. On paper, I was an unremarkable candidate. But interviews were a different story.

I'll never forget one of my first job interviews with a marketing firm that specialized in international clients. The interviewer, a polished woman in her forties, started with the standard questions about my education and career goals. Then she glanced down at my resume, and her eyebrows lifted slightly.

"I see you spent some time in Brazil during high school," she noted. "Tell me about that."

What followed wasn't really an interview anymore—it was a conversation. I told her about selling 2,000 calendars to fund my exchange year, about navigating favelas to get to soccer practice, about learning Portuguese through total immersion. She leaned forward, asking follow-up questions, genuinely engaged.

"And then you interned in Germany?" she continued, moving down my resume.

I shared stories about working with sales teams across Europe, about uncovering the human dynamics that affected the company's operations, and about adapting to different business cultures. Again, her interest was palpable.

When the formal interview ended, she walked me to the elevator, still asking questions about my experiences. "We'll be in touch soon," she said warmly. Two days later, I had an offer.

This pattern repeated itself in interview after interview. My resume would get me in the door, but my stories would get me the offer. Companies that initially seemed hesitant about my academic record became enthusiastic once they heard about Brazil and Germany.

What I was discovering—though I wouldn't have articulated it this way at the time—was the power of a compelling personal narrative. In a sea of candidates with similar degrees and comparable GPAs, I had something different: a story that made people lean in and listen.

My resume wasn't particularly impressive, but when I talked about learning to do business across cultural and linguistic barriers, about adapting to unfamiliar environments, about navigating complex human systems, suddenly I wasn't just another business graduate. I was someone who had already proven my ability to function effectively in the international business world.

During one particularly competitive interview for a global consulting firm, the hiring manager was direct: "Your grades aren't as strong as some other candidates we're considering. Why should we choose you?"

I acknowledged the truth of his assessment, then responded: "Because I've already done what consulting firms train their new hires to do—I've worked across cultures, analyzed human systems, and found solutions that technical analysis alone couldn't provide. I didn't learn these skills from textbooks; I learned them through direct experience in Brazil and Germany."

It wasn't arrogance—it was an accurate assessment of the value I could bring. The manager nodded thoughtfully, and I received an offer the following week.

By the time graduation rolled around, I had multiple job offers from reputable companies. None were at the executive level, of course—I'd be starting at the bottom like any new graduate—but the doors were open wider than my academic record alone would have justified.

On graduation day, as we sat in our caps and gowns under the Florida sun, I reflected on the unexpected path that had brought me to this moment. If you'd told me in high school that my decision (or my mom pushing me) to sell calendars door-to-door would ultimately help me land competitive jobs after college, I wouldn't have believed you. If you'd told me that my time getting lost in Brazilian public transportation would become a selling point in corporate interviews, I would have laughed.

Yet here I was, about to receive my degree, with job offers that many of my more academically accomplished classmates would have envied. Not because I was smarter or more talented, but because I had stories that set me apart—stories of challenges faced and overcome, of adaptability in unfamiliar environments, of seeing patterns others missed.

After the ceremony, my parents hosted a small celebration at Olive Garden with my roommate Dan (aka "Little Champ") and his family—nothing fancy, but special by our family's generally modest standards. My father raised his glass (Coca-Cola, since he didn't drink in public) for a toast: "To Alex, who has always found his own path."

In that moment, surrounded by family who had supported my unconventional choices, I felt a profound sense of validation. The different backpack I'd been born with—the one that meant selling calendars instead of asking my parents for money, the one that taught me the value of hard work and resilience from an early age—had become an unexpected asset.

But my father, ever the wise pastor, added something that would prove prophetic: "Remember that success isn't about titles or salaries. It's about finding work that lets you be fully yourself. It's about purpose, Alex." My dad always said he felt a 'calling' to The Byfield Parish Church and his career. He never pushed for anything…he answered the call and opened the doors God put before him.

I nodded, but I'm not sure I fully absorbed his meaning. At twenty-one, freshly graduated and fielding multiple job offers, my definition of success was still heavily influenced by the trappings I'd glimpsed during my German internship—prestigious positions, international travel, expense accounts, and the respect that seemed to come with corporate titles. And most importantly: money. I was obsessed with making money, simply because I never had money growing up.

Speaking of those job offers, I faced a decision: which position to accept? Looking back, this was a more pivotal choice than I recognized at the time. The offers varied in location, responsibilities, and compensation. Some involved travel, others were more office-based. Some were with American companies with international divisions, others with foreign companies operating in the U.S.

In making my decision, I focused on what seemed like the logical criterion: Which offer came with the highest salary? After growing up with limited means and taking on student loans, financial security felt like the responsible priority. And I was like a greedy kid. I wanted to be rich.

## Salary Over Satisfaction

The answer to that question led me to accept a position as a market analyst with a French company based back on the North Shore of Boston in the town of North Andover. The role involved analyzing sales trends for various European product lines, generating reports, and making recommendations to sales teams. The salary was about 15% higher than my next best offer—a marketing position with a smaller company in Florida.

On paper, it was the "best" offer. European company: check. International focus: check. Highest salary: check. I could already see myself in sleek meeting rooms like the ones in Germany, making strategic recommendations to executives, traveling to Paris for quarterly reviews.

I called to accept the position, feeling a surge of accomplishment as I did. This was it—the official start of my corporate career. My parents were proud, my college friends were impressed. I had successfully bridged the gap from blue-collar kid to international business professional.

Or so I thought.

What I didn't understand yet—what would become painfully clear in the months ahead—was that I had made my decision based on entirely the wrong criteria. I'd prioritized salary and prestige over alignment with my actual strengths and interests. I'd chosen a role that existed primarily behind a computer screen, analyzing data and creating reports, when my natural talents lay in reading people and connecting disparate ideas.

As I packed my belongings and prepared to move back to Massachusetts, I was filled with optimism about the path ahead. I didn't know that I was about to learn one of the most valuable lessons of my career: that success on someone else's terms isn't success at all, and that sometimes you have to get completely lost before you can find your way forward.

But that realization was still months away. For now, I was a newly minted international business graduate with an impressive job title and the highest starting salary among my friend group. By the conventional metrics of post-college success, I was crushing it.

What I couldn't have articulated then—but understand clearly now—is that the greatest gift from my unconventional journey wasn't the job offers or starting salary. It was the discovery of a truth that would eventually shape every aspect of my career: Your story is your most valuable asset. Not your GPA, not your technical skills, not even your experience in the conventional sense—but the unique narrative that explains how you see the world and what you bring to the table that no one else can.

In those job interviews, without fully realizing it, I had begun to harness the power of my story. I had learned to articulate the value of experiences that didn't fit neatly on a resume but had profoundly shaped my capabilities. This skill—the ability to craft and communicate a compelling personal narrative—would prove far more durable and valuable than any specific business knowledge I acquired in college.

It's a lesson I now share with every student I meet: Your credentials may get you considered, but your story is what gets you remembered. And in a world of increasing standardization and automation, being genuinely memorable is a competitive advantage no algorithm can replicate.

As I left Jacksonville behind, embarking on what I believed would be a straightforward ascent up the corporate ladder, I had no idea how soon that ladder would begin to feel like the completely wrong structure to climb. But that's the beauty of a good story—the most interesting parts often come when you think you've figured out the plot, only to discover you're in a different narrative altogether.

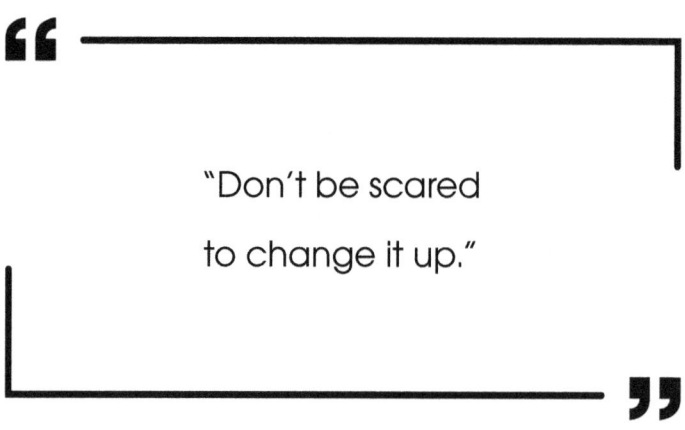

"Don't be scared to change it up."

# 9

# CHASING MONEY, FINDING MISERY

Boston in winter is a particular kind of misery. The wind whips off the Atlantic with a bitterness that seems personal, as if the city itself is offended by your presence. The snow doesn't so much fall as attack, driven horizontally by gusts that find every gap in your clothing. By January, the initial charm of New England winter has long since surrendered to the grim reality of four more months of cold, dark survival.

I'd forgotten this during my years in Florida. As I trudged to work every day, I couldn't help but compare the gray slush beneath my boots to the warm sand I'd left behind in Jacksonville. The contrast wasn't just meteorological; it was metaphorical.

## The Corporate Reality Check

My position at this new company looked impressive on paper. I was technically a "Market Analyst for North American Operations." The salary was exactly what I'd hoped for, significantly more than what my friends who'd stayed in Florida were making. The company had a global footprint, prestigious clients, and a nice office in North Andover, MA—an upscale corner of the North Shore.

It should have been perfect. It wasn't.

My first clue came during training. I sat in a conference room with other new analysts as a senior manager walked us through our responsibilities. She pulled up a slide showing a complex market analysis with colorful charts and precise-looking data visualizations.

"This is the kind of output we're looking for," she explained, gesturing to the screen. Then she added something that made me pause: "Remember, even if the numbers aren't quite right, as long as the charts look pretty, the executives will be happy."

I glanced around, expecting other new hires to share my confusion. Was she joking? But the others were nodding, taking notes. This was apparently standard operating procedure.

That moment should have been a red flag, but I rationalized it. Every company has its quirks, right? This was a multi-billion-dollar corporation—surely they didn't actually prioritize appearance over accuracy. I must have misunderstood.

I hadn't.

My day-to-day work quickly fell into a monotonous rhythm. I'd collect data on market trends for various product lines, input the numbers into spreadsheets, generate charts and graphs, and compile everything into reports that I presented to the sales team and then moved up the corporate hierarchy. Sometimes I'd receive feedback, usually about the presentation rather than the substance. "Make this chart pop more." "Can we get this in 3D?" "The executives prefer blue—can you change the color scheme?"

Rarely did anyone question the methodology or the implications of the data. It became clear that these reports weren't driving strategic decisions—they were props in a corporate theater, where the appearance of data-driven management was more important than the reality.

My desk was in a sea of cubicles on the 3rd floor, with a view of a parking lot. My colleagues were pleasant but distant. I made two great friends (Jaimie and Chiara). But everyone else seemed to exist in their own isolated world of spreadsheets and reports, with minimal interaction beyond obligatory small talk about weather and weekend plans. And, aside from Jaimie and Chiara, I was so much younger than everyone. I think most of my colleagues were more interested in the stories I would share from my weekend adventures than the work we were actually trying to accomplish at the company.

I kept waiting for the excitement to kick in—the strategic discussions, the cross-cultural negotiations, the sense of building something meaningful. I kept waiting to feel like the professional I'd glimpsed in Germany, the one contributing insights that actually mattered.

What I got instead were days that crawled by with excruciating slowness. I found myself checking the clock constantly. 9:17. 9:23. 9:36. How was it possible that only 19 minutes had passed? How would I survive until 5:00?

The cubicle environment was soul-crushing in ways I hadn't anticipated. The fluorescent lights cast everyone in the same unflattering pallor. The recycled air carried the mixed scents of coffee, printer toner, and microwave popcorn. The constant low hum of keyboards, phones, and hushed conversations created a white noise that somehow amplified the essential emptiness of the environment.

This was so far from what I'd experienced in Germany. There had been energy there, purpose, movement. Here, everything felt static—reports generated, filed, forgotten. Repeat.

My supervisor, Jean-Luc, was competent but uninspiring. Our weekly check-ins followed the same script. He'd ask if I'd completed my assignments, offer a few minor corrections, then dismiss me with a distracted "Keep up the good work." I don't think he could have picked me out of a lineup of two people.

I remember one day, three months in, I found myself standing in the bathroom on the third floor (pale as a ghost from the long winter), staring at my reflection in the mirror. "What are you doing here?" I asked myself. The face looking back had lost something—the spark, the curiosity, the sense of possibility that had defined me throughout college. I looked tired, and not just from lack of sleep.

The money, which had seemed so impressive when I accepted the offer, no longer justified the soul-deadening reality of the job. Yes, I could pay my bills and make my student loan payments with a bit left over, but at what cost? I was spending the majority of my waking hours doing work that felt meaningless, in an environment that drained rather than energized me, surrounded by people who seemed resigned to the same fate.

This wasn't the career I'd imagined. This wasn't even close.

The contrast with my experiences in Brazil and Germany was stark. In those places, I'd been constantly challenged, constantly learning, constantly engaged with people and ideas that expanded my understanding of the world. Even when things were difficult—navigating a foreign city, communicating across language barriers, adapting to unfamiliar business cultures—the difficulties felt worthwhile because they were in service of growth.

Here, the difficulties—mind-numbing tasks, bureaucratic absurdities, political maneuvering—seemed to serve no purpose beyond maintaining a system that existed primarily to perpetuate itself.

I tried to make it work. I volunteered for additional projects, hoping to find something more engaging. I reached out to colleagues in other departments, looking for connections or opportunities. I even pitched ideas for improving our market analysis methodology, thinking perhaps I could create more meaning in my current role.

None of it helped. The additional projects were just more of the same. The colleagues in other departments were equally disenchanted. My methodological improvements were acknowledged politely and promptly ignored.

And then there was the weather. Winter dragged on, gray and relentless. I missed the sun of Florida, the warmth, the light. I'd check the temperature in Jacksonville—75 and sunny—while scraping ice off my windshield in the numbing pre-dawn darkness. It felt like a metaphor for the wrong turn my life had taken.

One particularly bleak February morning, I sat at my desk preparing yet another market analysis that I knew would be skimmed, commented on for its visual appeal, and filed away. My supervisor walked by, paused, and peered over my shoulder.

"That chart needs to be prettier," she said, pointing to my screen. "The executives like pretty charts."

Something in me snapped. Not outwardly—I nodded politely and assured her I'd make it prettier—but internally, a decision crystallized. This wasn't just a bad fit or a temporary adjustment period. This was a fundamental mismatch between who I was and what this job demanded.

I'd made a serious error in my post-graduation decision-making. I'd prioritized salary over alignment with my strengths and interests. I'd chosen prestige over purpose. I'd opted for what looked good on paper rather than what would feel good in practice.

The realization was both liberating and terrifying. Liberating because it meant this misery was not my inevitable fate—I could make a different choice. Terrifying because I had no clear idea what that different choice should be. Plus, I'd committed to two years at this job, and I wasn't even a year in.

## A Call That Changes Everything

That evening, Mike Johnson, one of the former soccer coaches at Jacksonville University, called me to ask me to come play soccer there. He dropped a bombshell: "By the way, we still have your final year of soccer eligibility. At the time, NCAA rules allowed five academic years to play four seasons of soccer, and you only played three (due to my time in Germany away from Jacksonville). Due to a few NCAA violations the soccer program went through, the team had lost many of its key recruits to other colleges. Mike said, Why don't I offer you a full ride. Come back to Jacksonville and play your last year of eligibility, and you can get your MBA paid for."

The offer hit me like a ray of sunshine breaking through Boston's perpetual cloud cover. A chance to return to the warmth of Florida. A chance to get back on the soccer field. A chance to continue my education without adding to my debt. A chance to escape this corporate prison I'd locked myself into.

It seemed too good to be true. And in some ways, it was—as I would soon discover—but in that moment, it represented a lifeline I desperately needed.

"I'll think about it," I told Coach Johnson, but we both knew I'd already made up my mind.

The next day at work, I found myself mentally cataloging the things I wouldn't miss: the fluorescent lighting, the soul-crushing cubicle, the meaningless reports, the pretty charts that no one really cared about, the icy commute, the general sense of purposelessness that pervaded every hour.

The list of things I would miss was significantly shorter. Actually, it was nonexistent.

Two weeks later, I submitted my resignation, giving the standard two weeks' notice. Jean-Luc seemed surprised but not particularly concerned.

"Where are you going?" he asked, more out of curiosity than genuine interest.

"Back to Florida," I said. "I'm going to get my MBA and finish my soccer eligibility."

He nodded vaguely, already mentally moving on to other matters. "Well, good luck with that."

My last day at this job was unremarkable. A few colleagues signed a kind, good-luck card and had a cake in the break room. I turned in my badge, packed up the few personal items from my desk, and walked out into the July afternoon. I didn't look back.

As I left the building for the last time, I felt none of the anxiety or regret that conventional wisdom suggests should accompany such a seemingly impulsive career move. Instead, I felt an overwhelming sense of relief—as if I'd been holding my breath for over a year and could finally exhale.

I had made a mistake in coming back to Boston, in choosing this job based primarily on salary, in trying to fit myself into a conventional corporate mold. But the greater mistake would have been staying out of fear or inertia, or concern for how my resume would look.

That night, as I packed up, preparing for the drive back to Florida, I came across the journal I'd kept during my time in Brazil. Flipping through it, I found an entry from my first month there, when everything was overwhelming and I questioned whether I could actually adapt to such a different environment.

The words resonated with my current situation. Once again, I was venturing into unfamiliar territory—walking away from the security of a corporate job to pursue something less conventional, less certain, but potentially more aligned with who I actually was.

As I loaded my car the next morning, ready to begin the long drive south, I realized I'd learned a crucial lesson: Don't be scared to change it up. The path forward isn't always the one that looks most impressive or offers the highest initial salary. Sometimes it's the one that makes space for your actual strengths to flourish, even if that path seems unconventional to others.

My journey back to Florida was both an ending and a beginning—the conclusion of my brief, miserable corporate experiment and the start of something new, something that I couldn't yet define but that somehow felt right despite its uncertainty.

Little did I know that this decision—this willingness to abandon the conventional path to follow my instincts—would set in motion a chain of events that would lead me to opportunities I couldn't possibly have imagined while sitting in that gray cubicle in Boston.

"Sometimes the most important doors open only after others have closed."

# 10

# A (QUICK) RETURN TO COLLEGE

As I drove south on I-95, putting mile after mile between myself and Boston, I could feel the weight lifting with each state line I crossed. New York. New Jersey. Maryland. Virginia. With each southward mile, the temperature rose a few degrees, and my spirits along with it.

My car was packed with everything I owned, which wasn't much. I'd given away furniture and kitchen items, keeping only clothes, books, and a few mementos from Brazil and Germany. There's something liberating about fitting your life into a single vehicle, about the tangible lightness of fewer possessions.

**A Second Chance**

I had no apartment lined up in Jacksonville, no detailed plan beyond Coach Johnson's offer. By conventional metrics, I was taking a significant step backward—from salaried professional to graduate student and soccer player. But it didn't feel like regression. It felt like a correction.

This was the year 2000—a time of cultural optimism and economic boom. The dot-com bubble hadn't yet burst, and unconventional career paths were becoming more acceptable. But still, walking away from a corporate job after less than a year to go back to school and play soccer wasn't exactly a move from the standard career playbook.

I didn't care. I'd tried the standard playbook, and it had nearly suffocated me.

Meanwhile, something else was happening in American culture that would intersect with my life in ways I couldn't have predicted. A new type of television show called *Survivor* had premiered, capturing the nation's imagination with its blend of outdoor challenges, strategic gameplay, and interpersonal drama. The idea of ordinary people facing extraordinary circumstances resonated with viewers—and with me.

I'd always been drawn to challenges that tested physical and mental resilience. My experiences in Brazil and Germany have taught me that I thrived in situations that required adaptability and social intelligence. Watching the early episodes of *Survivor*, I thought, "I need to do that."

On a whim, I sent in an audition tape months ago. It was nothing fancy—just me talking to the camera about my background, my love of adventure, but stuck in a corporate job that was suffocating me, and why I thought I'd be a good contestant. I didn't expect anything to come of it, but it felt good to put myself out there for something that genuinely excited me.

While I was driving through North Carolina, my cell phone rang. The screen showed an unfamiliar Los Angeles number. Curious, I answered.

"Is this Alex Boylan?" a woman's voice asked.

"Yes, that's me."

"This is Lynne from CBS casting. We received your audition tape for *Survivor* and we'd like to move forward with the next steps in the process."

I pulled the car over immediately. My casual application had actually gotten attention?

"That's...that's great!" I managed. "What are the next steps?"

She explained the process: a more detailed application, a psychological evaluation, a physical fitness assessment, and eventually, if all went well, an in-person interview in Los Angeles. It was a lengthy process with no guarantees, but I had cleared the first major hurdle. She asked me a few questions about my job, which I mentioned in the casting tape. And I replied, 'Well...I quit that job and am headed back to college for my MBA. She paused and said 'Grad Student. That's a bit different than the story in your casting tape, but we would like to move to the next casting step with you. As you can imagine, I was ecstatic. For the rest of the drive, all I could think about was being on that island playing *Survivor*. But I needed to get my head in gear. This was a long shot, and I had a bird in hand. An awesome offer at Jacksonville University with a team that was expecting me. I tossed it up to God…and said…let me know where you want all this to go.

When I arrived in Jacksonville, Coach Johnson welcomed me back with his characteristic blend of warmth and friendly coaching demeanor.

"Have you had time to get yourself back in game shape?" he asked during our first meeting in his office. "You are going to be the elder on this squad, so we will be looking to you for leadership."

One season of soccer and my MBA paid for. Seemed like a great deal to me :)

It sounded perfect—a chance to continue my education while getting back on the soccer field and away from fluorescent-lit cubicles. I signed the paperwork that day and enrolled in classes for the fall semester.

Training for my final pre-season of collegiate soccer also felt right. The discipline of multiple daily practices, the camaraderie of teammates, the simple joy of playing a sport I loved—these things had been missing from my life in Boston, and their return felt like recovering a vital part of myself.

## Plans Fall Apart

One week into pre-season training at Jacksonville, Coach Johnson and the Athletic director walked onto the pitch and summoned me over. Coach Johnson's expression was uncharacteristically serious with a sense of sadness.

"There's a problem with your eligibility, Alex," he said without preamble. "The NCAA has made you ineligible to play." The five-year clock starts from when you first enrolled, making this 'technically' my sixth year since I played my freshman year.

I sat there, trying to process what this meant. "So I can't play my final year?"

He shook his head. "Not according to their ruling. You can appeal, but these decisions rarely get overturned, especially with the recruiting violations the program received the year prior. And unfortunately, we can't give you that full scholarship we promised."

Just like that, my reason for returning to Jacksonville evaporated. I could continue the MBA program, but without the full-ride scholarship.

This felt like I got hit with a brick. I'd just quit my stable corporate job for this MBA opportunity. But I still had a sliver of hope—I still had this *Survivor* show interested in me. So I decided to hang around Jacksonville to see how things played out.

Each time I advanced to the next round, the possibility became more real. Could I actually end up on this show that had captured the nation's attention? The idea was thrilling!

The casting team seemed particularly interested in my background—the blue-collar kid who'd sold calendars to get to Brazil, who'd worked his way through challenging environments, who'd left a corporate job to follow a less conventional path. My story resonated with them in much the same way it had resonated with job interviewers.

"You're different from our typical applicants," one casting director told me during a phone interview. "Most people either have the survival skills or the social game, but your international experiences suggest you might have both."

As the *Survivor* possibility seemed to gain momentum, and less than two weeks from losing the scholorship, the deadly call came from CBS.

"Alex, we're very interested in you for the show," Lynne said. "But why are you lying to us?"

"What are you talking about?" I replied. "We checked with Jacksonville University," she said, "and you are NOT a registered MBA student." I tried to explain the events that had transpired, and that I lost my ride, etc.

Even though it was all 100% the truth, Lynne said. "I'm sorry, Alex, we really like you, but this isn't adding up. We are going in a different direction.

I was not going on *Survivor*.

My heart sank. I can't remember what I said exactly, but I pushed for her to reconsider. "Alex, we are moving on," she said. That was it.

So in less than two weeks, I went from a corporate job that suffocated me, to the excitement of going back to school and playing soccer, to getting a call from *Survivor* saying they were interested in me for the show, to losing my scholarship on a technicality, to *Survivor* rejecting me.

Within the span of less than two weeks, both paths I'd been pursuing simultaneously—*Survivor* and a return to collegiate soccer—had collapsed. The neat life I'd been rebuilding was suddenly in shambles.

That evening, feeling adrift, I called Chris Luca, my best friend since kindergarten. He was finishing his engineering degree at Clemson University and always gave me a clear-eyed perspective when I needed it most.

"So you're telling me your corporate job didn't work out, you can't play soccer at JU, and *Survivor* rejected you," he summarized after I explained my situation. "Sounds like life is going well for you, bro," throwing some humor at me in the midst of this chaos.

But what now? Do I just focus on the MBA and find another way to pay for it? Do I look for another corporate job, even though I hated the last one? Do I try something completely different?"

"Well," Chris said thoughtfully, "what do you actually want? Not what looks good on paper or what makes logical sense—what would make you genuinely happy right now?"

It was a simple question, but a profound one. What did I actually want?

Not another corporate cubicle, that was certain. Not just any job that paid well. Not even necessarily the MBA, if I were being completely honest with myself. That had been part of a package deal with soccer, and without the athletic component, it lost a bit of its appeal.

What I wanted was what I'd always wanted: adventure, challenge, human connection, the chance to test my limits in new environments. I wanted sunshine and mobility and the feeling of being fully alive that had been so conspicuously absent in that Boston office.

And then it hit me—an idea so ridiculous and perfect that it made me laugh out loud.

"Chris," I said, "remember that movie *Cocktail*? The one with Tom Cruise?"

"Sure," he replied, sounding confused by the abrupt change of subject. "What about it?"

"Remember how he goes to Jamaica to tend bar? Live on the beach, make good money, no corporate BS?"

There was a pause, then Chris started laughing too. "Are you serious? You want to be a bartender in the Caribbean?"

"Why not?" The more I thought about it, the more appealing it became. "I have no commitments right now. I could go somewhere warm, learn a new skill, meet interesting people, figure out my next move without the pressure of a traditional career path."

"You're completely insane," Chris said, but I could hear the admiration in his voice. "Also, where would you go?"

I didn't even hesitate. "St. John. U.S. Virgin Islands. I've heard through my college buddy Dov's older brother Jessup (who did this) that bartenders there make serious money during tourist season, and you don't need a work visa since it's a U.S. territory."

## Learning the Art of Service

The idea had appeared fully formed, as if it had been waiting in the wings of my consciousness. It wasn't conventional or prestigious. It wouldn't advance my corporate resume. My former colleagues in Boston would probably see it as confirmation that I couldn't hack it in the "real world."

But it felt right in a way that was becoming increasingly important to me—the internal compass of authenticity rather than the external validation of conventional success.

Within days, the decision crystallized. I would drive to Clemson to leave my car with Chris, and fly to St. John with nothing but a backpack and the little savings I had left from my Boston job.

I called my parents and they were…well…cautiously intrigued. Although my mom says to this day that she was worried about that move and wondered what I was thinking. My parents were less immediately supportive when I called to tell them. After all, they'd raised me to value education and professional achievement. The idea of their son abandoning corporate opportunities and graduate studies to mix drinks on a beach seemed a bit irresponsible.

## A (QUICK) RETURN TO COLLEGE

"Are you sure about this, Alex?" my father asked, concern evident in his voice. "This seems...impulsive."

"It is impulsive," I admitted. "But I also think it's right. I need to figure some things out, and doing that in a beautiful place while making good money seems like a reasonable approach."

My mother was quiet for a moment, then said, "You've always found your way, even when your path looked different from everyone else's. I pray you'll find it again, Alex."

Her words were exactly what I needed to hear—not blanket approval, but acknowledgment that my unconventional choices had led to growth before, and might do so again.

As I packed my backpack—the same one that had accompanied me to Brazil, through Europe, and to Germany—I felt that familiar mix of terror and exhilaration that had preceded my biggest growth experiences. I was leaping into the unknown again, trusting that I'd figure it out as I went.

The corporate world had demanded that I become someone I wasn't. The return to college athletics had been blocked by bureaucratic rules. The *Survivor* opportunity had slipped through my fingers. But this path—unexpected, unconventional, perfectly imperfect path to St. John—was entirely mine to create.

I had no idea then how this seemingly random decision would connect to future opportunities, how the skills and relationships I'd develop on that island would play into later chapters of my story. I just knew that after months of trying to force myself into roles that didn't fit, I was finally choosing a path that felt authentically mine, however crazy it might look from the outside.

Standing at the curb of Charlotte's Airport, where Chris had accompanied me, I handed him the keys to my car. It wasn't much—a used Ford Explorer with high mileage and a temperamental air conditioner—but it represented the last vestige of my conventional life. My worldly possessions had been whittled down to what fit in my backpack: some clothes, a few books, my passport, and a few credit cards I was floating on.

"You sure about this?" Chris asked, jingling the keys. "Once you get on that plane, you're committed, bro."

I looked at the backpack at my feet. "I think that's the point."

Chris shook his head, but he was smiling. "Only you would lose a corporate job, lose a scholarship, and get rejected from a reality show, all in the same month, then decide the solution is to become a bartender on some Caribbean island where you don't know a single person."

When he put it that way, it did sound slightly unhinged. But the strange thing was, none of those setbacks felt like failures to me. They felt like course corrections, pushing me toward a path that was somehow right, even if I couldn't fully articulate why.

"I'll be back for your graduation," I promised, shouldering my backpack. "Save me a couch to crash on."

Sometimes the most important doors open only after others have closed. I was about to discover that St. John awaited—and with it, the next unexpected turn in a journey that was proving anything but predictable.

As I prepared to board a flight to Puerto Rico, then to St. Thomas (the gateway to St. John), I felt none of the hesitation that had nagged at me when I accepted the Boston job. Despite the objective insecurity of becoming a bartender with limited experience on an island where I knew no one, the decision felt right in a way that defied logical explanation.

Sometimes, I was learning that the best decisions aren't the ones that look sensible on paper. They're the ones that resonate with your authentic self, that create space for growth even—or especially—when the path forward isn't clearly marked.

St. John awaited—and with it, the next unexpected chapter in a journey that had already taught me to trust the process, even when the destination wasn't clear.

"Align your choices with your actual values rather than external expectations."

# 11

# AN ISLAND, A BACKPACK, AND NO PLAN B

Island life has its own rhythm, distinct from the manufactured urgency of the corporate world. In St. John, time was measured not by quarterly reports or project deadlines but by the sunrise, the ferry schedule, the ebb and flow of tourists, and the nightly ritual of sunset.

After securing my position at Woody's and finding permanent housing, I settled into this new rhythm with surprising ease. The transition from market analyst to bartender might seem dramatic on paper, but the reality was liberating. Each day had clear boundaries—I worked my shift, gave it my full attention and energy, and when it ended, I was truly done. No emails to check, no reports to prepare at home, no anxiety about tomorrow's presentation.

Woody's slogan—"Best Happy Hour in the Virgin Islands"—wasn't just marketing. From 3-6 PM daily, the open-air bar became the center of Cruz Bay's social life. Locals mixed with tourists, fishing guides chatted with investment bankers on vacation, and permanent residents welcomed seasonal workers into the fold of island society.

My role in this daily ritual evolved quickly. The learning curve was steep—memorizing dozens of cocktail recipes, developing the coordination to mix drinks efficiently, learning to engage with customers while keeping track of multiple orders—but I thrived in the challenge.

"You're good with people," Todd observed one evening as I chatted with a group of tourists while simultaneously making their complicated drink order. "They trust you. That's not something I can teach."

It was a simple observation, but it resonated deeply. Throughout my life—from selling those calendars door-to-door to navigate my way through Brazil, to uncovering human dynamics during my German internship—my ability to connect with people has been a consistent strength. Here at Woody's, that same skill was directly valuable in a way it never had been in that Boston cubicle.

The financial aspect of island life surprised me most. I'd accepted the bartending path, assuming it would mean a significant pay cut from my corporate salary. I was prepared for that trade-off, valuing freedom and location over income. But a curious thing happened: I started making more money than I ever had in Boston.

## When Less Becomes More

The math was simple but counterintuitive. My hourly wage was modest, but tips during tourist season were substantial. On a busy night at the bar, I could make several hundred dollars in tips alone. Working five or six shifts a week, my income far surpassed what I'd earned as a market analyst, with significantly fewer hours and without the soul-crushing stress. And no taxes.

What's more, my expenses were lower. Yes, island living came with its premiums—groceries shipped from the mainland were expensive, and housing wasn't cheap—but I no longer needed professional clothes, a car, or many of the trappings that had devoured my Boston paycheck. My apartment was basic but sufficient, my wardrobe consisted mainly of t-shirts and shorts, and entertainment involved beaches, hiking trails, and dinners with friends rather than expensive outings.

Within three months of arriving on St. John, I had paid off the credit card debt that had followed me from Boston and started building savings for the first time since college. The financial freedom was unexpected and empowering. I wasn't rich by any conventional standard, but I had enough to live comfortably and save for whatever might come next, all while working in a place most people only got to visit on vacation.

"This is the secret they don't tell you in college," said Mike, a fellow bartender who'd left a law career in Chicago five years earlier. "You don't need a prestigious job to live well. You need to understand the relationship between what you earn, what you spend, and how you value your time."

It was a basic principle of economics reframed in human terms. In Boston, I'd earned a "good" salary but spent most of it maintaining a lifestyle I didn't particularly enjoy. In St. John, I earned more working fewer hours, spent less on things that didn't matter to me, and ended up with both more money and more life satisfaction.

The work itself taught me lessons no business school ever could. Bartending is fundamentally about service, about making people happy. It's also about efficiency, multitasking, conflict resolution, and reading social cues. On a busy night, I might serve a hundred different customers—from the wealthy yacht owner to the local fisherman, from the honeymooning couple to the long-term expat—each requiring a slightly different approach.

I learned to defuse tension between rowdy tourists and annoyed locals. I developed an eye for spotting potential problems before they escalated. I mastered the art of the genuine conversation that made customers feel welcome while still serving everyone efficiently. These skills weren't listed on my international business degree, but they were invaluable human capabilities that would serve me in any future endeavor.

"You're not just serving drinks," Todd told me during a quiet afternoon shift. "You're selling an experience. People might forget what they ordered, but they'll remember how you made them feel."

That insight—that most business is ultimately about how you make people feel—was profound in its simplicity. It applied as much to high-level corporate strategy as it did to mixing a perfect painkiller cocktail. The difference was that at Woody's, I could see the results immediately in smiles and tips rather than waiting for quarterly performance reviews.

Beyond the bar, island life offered its own education. St. John, with its limited resources and isolated position, required resilience and adaptability. Power outages were common. Water came from cisterns that collected rainwater, making conservation essential. When supplies ran low in island stores, you simply did without until the next shipment arrived.

Living with these constraints was a daily exercise in problem-solving and flexibility—skills I'd developed in Brazil and Germany but honed to new levels on the island. When the power went out during dinner rush, you didn't panic; you served drinks by flashlight and turned it into part of the island experience. When a tropical storm prevented ferry crossings, you didn't complain about missed deliveries; you improvised with what you had.

The natural beauty of the island became an integral part of my daily life. I'd wake early to swim at Trunk Bay before the tourists arrived, watching sea turtles glide beneath me in crystal-clear water. On days off, I'd hike the island's trails, discovering hidden beaches and ruins of old sugar plantations reclaimed by the forest. Sunset became a sacred ritual, a moment to pause and appreciate the extraordinary place I found myself in.

This daily immersion in nature balanced the intensity of work in a busy bar. The quiet mornings in the ocean and the vibrant nights serving crowds created a yin and yang that felt sustainable in a way my previous work life never had.

The community I found on St. John was unlike any I'd experienced before. Island society had its own unwritten rules and values. Status wasn't determined by job titles or possessions but by character, reliability, and contribution to the community. The millionaire who treated locals with respect was welcomed; the wealthy tourist who behaved arrogantly was merely tolerated. The person who showed up to help when a neighbor's roof leaked during a storm earned more social capital than someone with an impressive resume.

This value system resonated with me. It aligned with what I'd always intuitively felt but had never seen so clearly embodied in a community. Success wasn't about climbing ladders or accumulating credentials—it was about building meaningful connections, contributing value, and living authentically.

My circle of friends expanded beyond my coworkers to include an eclectic mix of island residents: Kenny, a former Wall Street trader who now ran a charter boat; Maria, an artist who created stunning seascapes sold in local galleries; Dave, a contractor who'd built half the homes on the island; and Rebekah, a marine biologist studying coral reef restoration. Each had their own story of how they'd found their way to St. John, often involving a rejection of conventional paths similar to my own.

"Most people here are running either to something or from something," Rebekah observed one evening as a group of us watched the sunset from a lookout point. "The interesting ones are doing both at the same time."

Her words captured something essential about the island community. We were all, in some sense, refugees from mainstream expectations, seeking different measures of success and fulfillment. Yet we weren't merely escaping—we were also moving toward a vision of life that valued presence, connection, and direct experience over abstraction and accumulation.

As my time on the island progressed, I found myself increasingly respected within this community. I was no longer just the newcomer with a funny Boston accent, but a recognized part of the island ecosystem. Locals greeted me by name as I walked through Cruz Bay. I was invited to community events, late-night bonfires on the beach, and the insider gatherings that tourists never saw.

This sense of belonging was deeply satisfying. Yet even as I felt increasingly integrated into island life, I remained aware that this was a chapter rather than the complete story. The restlessness that had driven me from Brazil to Germany to Boston to Jacksonville to St. John hadn't disappeared; it had merely quieted for a season.

When tourists would ask, as they inevitably did, "How long have you lived here?" and "Do you plan to stay forever?" my answers evolved over time. At first, I'd shrug and say I was figuring it out as I went. Later, I developed a more nuanced response: "I'll stay until I've learned what I came here to learn."

Though I couldn't have articulated exactly what that learning was, I recognized that St. John was teaching me essential lessons about what I valued, how I wanted to live, and what kind of work truly engaged me. The island was a classroom as much as a refuge.

By the time I received Chris's letter reminding me of his upcoming graduation and my car still parked at his place in Clemson, I had a clearer sense of what those lessons were. I'd learned that financial success and conventional prestige were poor substitutes for work that engaged my authentic strengths. I'd discovered that I thrived in environments that combined social connection with tangible results. I'd confirmed that my ability to build relationships across different backgrounds was a genuine asset, not just a soft skill to list on a resume.

Most importantly, I'd experienced firsthand the freedom that comes from aligning your choices with your actual values rather than external expectations. The path from Georgetown, Massachusetts, to Brazil to Germany to Jacksonville to St. John hadn't been linear or predictable, but each step had revealed something essential about who I was and what mattered to me.

As I prepared to leave the island—not because I had to, but because something told me it was time for the next chapter—I felt a profound gratitude for this unexpected detour. What had begun as an impulsive decision born of disappointment had become one of the most formative experiences of my life.

My last shift turned into an impromptu farewell party. Regulars showed up with small gifts and good wishes. Joe presented me with a t-shirt signed by the entire staff. Kenny promised to take me out on his boat whenever I returned to visit.

"You're always welcome back," Winston told me as we closed up that final night. "Not everyone finds their place here, but you did. That door's always open."

It meant more than he knew. In a life characterized by movement and change, the knowledge that I had a place where I truly belonged—even if I was choosing to leave it—was profoundly reassuring.

The morning I left St. John, I took one last swim at Trunk Bay at sunrise. Floating in that perfect turquoise water, watching the island wake up to another beautiful day, I felt a completeness I hadn't expected. I wasn't leaving because the island had failed me or because I was running from anything. I was leaving because this chapter had served its purpose, and somewhere—though I didn't know where yet—the next chapter was waiting to begin.

As the ferry pulled away from Cruz Bay dock, I stood at the railing watching the island recede. In my backpack was more than I'd arrived with—not just in terms of money saved, but in clarity gained, lessons learned, and connections formed. St. John had given me the most valuable gift possible: not an escape from reality, but a clearer vision of what reality could be when aligned with my authentic self.

I didn't know what awaited me on the mainland or what opportunity might present itself next. But I knew that I was ready—not because I had everything figured out, but because I had learned to trust the journey, even when the destination wasn't clear.

And sometimes, that's the most important freedom of all.

> "The real prize is clarity, a vivid glimpse of your path forward."

# 12

# *THE AMAZING RACE*

The drive from Clemson to Boston had a circular quality to it—retracing in reverse the journey I'd made when I fled corporate life for the Caribbean. But I was returning a different person than the one who had left. My skin was tanned from island sun, my hair lightened by salt water, and my perspective transformed by a year of living on St. John.

## A Pop-Up Ad Changes Everything

Chris had graduated with honors, a double engineering degree, securing him immediate job offers from prestigious firms. As we drove back to Boston together, he would share his excitement for the engineering job offers coming in.

"So what's the plan for you now, island boy?" he asked. "Back to the corporate world?"

I shook my head. "Honestly? I have no idea. But I've got some savings from bartending, and I figure something will present itself."

Chris laughed. "Only you would leave paradise without a plan."

"I've learned to trust the process," I replied, surprising myself with how genuine that sentiment had become.

Returning to the North Shore of Boston felt both strange and natural. Everything was unchanged, but my relationship to it had shifted. I no longer saw it as the site of my professional failure but simply as one chapter in a continuing story.

During those first weeks back in Massachusetts, I reconnected with old friends, helped my mother with projects around the house and church, and gave myself permission to exist without immediately replacing one identity with another. This wasn't denial or procrastination. It was a genuine trust in the process that had brought me this far.

After a few weeks at home, Chris and I were hanging out watching the Red Sox game at my parents' house while idly browsing the internet on their computer—this was 2001, when home internet was still relatively new and smartphones didn't exist. A pop-up ad appeared on the screen: "Do you have what it takes to race around the world for a million dollars?"

Normally, I would have clicked away from such an obvious gimmick (annoying pop-ups on your computer were common in these early days of the internet). But something about the wording caught my attention. I clicked for more information and discovered it was a casting call for the second season of a new reality competition show called "The Amazing Race."

The premise was simple yet captivating: teams of two would race around the world, completing challenges and navigating foreign countries, with the first team to reach the final destination winning a million-dollar prize. It combined travel, competition, cultural immersion, and problem-solving—elements that resonated with many of my core interests.

I looked over at Chris. We'd been best friends since kindergarten, had grown up together, and had maintained our connection despite different college paths. We'd always talked about traveling together someday. This could be that opportunity, with the added bonus of potentially winning life-changing money.

I called him over to the computer immediately. "Chris, check this out. A casting call for a show called *The Amazing Race*. It's teams of two racing around the world for a million dollars. We need to apply."

He paused. "You're serious?"

"Dead serious. It's perfect for us. You're detail-oriented and analytical; I'm good with people and adaptable. We've known each other forever, so our communication is solid. And we both want to see the world."

We asked my little sister Alexis to film us. We walked outside on my back deck and recorded our audition tape. The application required teams to explain why they should be selected and what made their relationship unique. We didn't have fancy recording equipment—just my dad's old

VHS camcorder. No elaborate setting either—just the back deck of my parents' house.

What we did have was genuine chemistry and a friendship that stretched back to childhood. We stood on the back deck, camera rolling, and simply talked about why we wanted this opportunity and what made us the right team for it.

"We've been best friends since we were five years old," Chris explained to the camera. "We can read each other's minds at this point."

"And we've always talked about traveling the world together," I added. "Chris is the planner, I'm the people person. We both came from small towns and went on to play Division 1 sports. Individually, we were both extremely competitive. Together, we're unstoppable."

We were relaxed, authentic, bantering back and forth with the easy rhythm of friends who don't need to impress each other. There were no rehearsed lines, no forced enthusiasm—just two guys who genuinely wanted an adventure together.

We mailed the tape to Los Angeles and promptly tried to forget about it. The odds of being selected seemed astronomical, and neither of us wanted to build up expectations only to face disappointment.

Weeks passed. Both of us lived at our parents' house, taking on fun, random summer jobs for money.

One day, while hanging out with Chris at our good friend Andrew's house, yes, the same Andrew's house whose father gave me that internship in Germany, Mike (who I worked for in Germany) told us he wanted his son to go on an adventure. "Alex, I have a proposition for you and Chris," he said. "I want my son Andrew to go on an adventure, to have a similar experience to what you had in Germany. You see this fence?" It was a massive property in Groveland that ran from the street down to the Merrimac River. "If you three paint this fence, I'll buy your flights to Europe."

We said yes. No hesitation. We spent every night for two weeks painting that fence. Then all three of us headed off to Europe—no cell phone, no plans, just a plane ticket in and out, with no care in the world.

At this time, my parents happened to have been given a few weeks at a friend's property in Switzerland. So after landing in Paris, we traveled a bit and then swung by there to check in. After a cheese fondue dinner and a game of Dutch Blitz (my mom's favorite), the phone rang. I can still hear my mom saying, "Where is the phone? I've never heard it ring since we have been here." My mom picked up. It was Chris's Mom. CBS is trying to find you two. They want to meet you two as potential contestants for *The Amazing Race*. Chris and I spoke privately. It was a bit awkward. We were in Europe thanks to our other buddy, Andrew, whose father bought us the plane tickets. How do we leave Andrew? But we both looked at each other and knew we would regret it if we didn't try, and we expected Andrew would do the same if the situation were reversed.

So we bee-lined to Rome (where we were supposed to leave for the States a few weeks later). We switched tickets to get home as soon as possible. Chris's mom left a car at Logan airport in Boston, so when we landed we could drive straight from Boston to New York City to make the interview.

What followed was a whirlwind of paperwork, phone interviews, medical examinations, and anxious waiting. Each time we cleared another hurdle in the casting process, the possibility became more real.

The final step was an in-person interview in Los Angeles. CBS flew us out, put us up in a hotel, and scheduled a series of meetings with producers, psychologists, and network executives.

Walking onto the CBS lot in Hollywood felt surreal. Just months earlier, I'd been tending bar on a small Caribbean island. Now I was being considered for a prime-time reality competition with a million-dollar prize.

The interviews were intense, probing our relationship, our motivations, our potential reactions to extreme stress and cultural disorientation. They wanted to know if we'd make good television, of course, but they also needed to ensure we could handle the physical and psychological demands of the race.

"You've traveled internationally before," one producer noted, looking at my background information. "Brazil, Germany, the Caribbean. How do you think that will help you in this competition?"

"It's taught me to be comfortable with discomfort," I replied honestly. "To see unfamiliarity as an opportunity rather than a threat. And to connect with people across language and cultural barriers."

Chris added, "And I bring the analytical skills to balance his people skills. He speaks Portuguese; I can read a map. Between us, we cover most of what you need to navigate the world effectively."

Back at Chris's house, we settled in to watch the first episode of the first season of *The Amazing Race*. Thirty minutes before the episode started, Chris's house phone rang. It was Lynne (yes, the same Lynne from *Survivor*) on the other end. "Are you two about to watch the show?" she asked. "I hope so, because congratulations—you've both been selected for Season 2 of *The Amazing Race*.

In the desert of Nevada, standing at the starting line of *The Amazing Race*, I felt a surge of emotions—adrenaline, excitement, anxiety, and a strange calm that came from knowing I was exactly where I was meant to be. Beside me stood Chris, equally focused on the adventure ahead. Around us were the other teams—strangers for now, but soon to become both competitors and companions in an experience few would ever understand.

When Phil Keoghan shouted "Go!" it was like being launched from a catapult. We sprinted to our backpacks, grabbed the first clue, and began a journey that would take us across continents, through extreme environments, and into some of the most extraordinary moments of my life.

The race was brutal in ways I hadn't fully anticipated. Sleep deprivation became our constant companion. We operated on adrenaline and determination, sometimes going 30+ hours without proper rest. The physical challenges—running with heavy packs, completing grueling tasks, enduring long flights—tested our limits daily.

But more challenging than the physical demands were the mental and emotional ones. Making rapid decisions with limited information. Navigating unfamiliar cities where we couldn't speak the language. Maintaining our partnership and friendship under extreme stress. These were the true tests of the race.

Chris and I had our moments of tension, of course. When exhaustion set in, tempers could flare. But our long history gave us an advantage—we knew each other's strengths and weaknesses intimately, and we had a shorthand communication developed over decades of friendship.

"You navigate, I'll translate," became our mantra in foreign countries. Chris had an engineer's mind for maps and spatial reasoning; I had the people skills to connect across language barriers. Together, we formed a more effective unit than either of us could have been individually.

As the race progressed and other teams were eliminated, I began to notice something unexpected: I was becoming as fascinated by the production of the show as by the competition itself. During brief moments of downtime, I found myself observing the producers, camera operators, and sound technicians with increasing interest.

This production team was accomplishing something remarkable: coordinating a complex, multi-continental race while capturing compelling television, all while remaining nearly invisible to viewers. They were storytellers using the entire world as their set, and I was mesmerized by their craft.

During a lengthy flight from Africa to Asia, I found myself seated near Joe, one of the producers. Against the rules, I struck up a conversation.

"How do you plan all this?" I asked, genuinely curious about the logistics behind the race.

Joe gave me a measured look. "You know we're not supposed to interact with contestants outside of structured situations."

"I know," I admitted. "But I'm fascinated by what you do. This isn't just a race for me—I'm seeing a whole career I never knew existed."

He softened slightly. "Eyes on the prize, Boylan. You're still in this competition."

"Of course," I said. "But when it's over, win or lose, I want to get a job like yours."

That brief exchange crystallized something for me. Yes, I wanted to win the million dollars desperately. But I'd also stumbled upon a potential career path that combined everything I loved: travel, storytelling, creating meaningful experiences, and connecting across cultures.

As teams continued to be eliminated and we advanced through the competition, the reality of potentially winning began to sink in. Chris and I had developed a rhythm and strategy that was working. We weren't always in first place, but we were consistently strong, avoiding the critical mistakes and those critical moments that sent other teams home.

Finally, we reached the final leg of the race. Only three teams remained, and we were one of them. The million dollars was tantalizingly close—just one more perfect leg away.

## Fifty Yards to a Million Dollars

The final moments of *The Amazing Race* remain frozen in my memory with crystal clarity. We were in San Francisco, the last leg of a journey that had taken us across continents, through extreme environments, and to the absolute limits of our endurance. Only two teams stood between us and the million-dollar prize—Blake and Paige and Tara and Wil, fierce competitors who had matched us step for step throughout the race.

The final challenge had us searching for clues in Fisherman's Wharf before making our way to the finish line at Fort Baker. We lost Blake and Page and didn't know if they were in front or behind us. Tara and Wil had a slight lead on us leaving the Wharf, but navigation through San Francisco's challenging streets could easily erase that advantage. Back and forth for the next hour of racing, Tara, Wil, Chris, and I exchanged positions. They were ahead, we were ahead. They tried to trick us by deviating to a random hillside, Chris and I back in front. Then behind. This continued…

When we finally arrived at the base of the hill leading to Fort Baker, we could see Tara and Wil's taxi pulling away, meaning they had the lead at this critical juncture. What followed was the most intense physical test of the entire race—a lung-burning, muscle-screaming uphill sprint with everything on the line.

I can still feel the gravel crunching under my shoes, hear Chris's labored breathing beside me, while chasing Tara and Wil, who probably had a two-hundred-yard lead on us. My legs felt like lead, but with each painful step, I thought about everything that had gotten us to this moment in life, both of us pushing our bodies and minds beyond their limits for weeks.

The final stretch came down to pure will. With maybe fifty yards to go, we had caught up to Tara and Wil. In that moment, Chris and I found a final surge of energy we didn't know we had. Side by side, we pushed forward, passing Tara and Will with maybe twenty yards to go before crossing the finish line mere seconds before our competitors.

The moment of victory was both explosive and dreamlike. Phil is declaring us the official winners. The eliminated contestants are cheering. Chris and I collapsed into an exhausted, ecstatic embrace. A million dollars was ours.

"We did it," Chris kept saying, his voice hoarse from exertion. "We did it."

The race had tested every aspect of our friendship. We'd seen each other at our worst—sleep-deprived, hungry, frustrated—and still managed to function as a team. If anything, the experience had strengthened a bond that was already decades strong.

But even in that moment of triumph, with confetti still settling around us, my mind was already moving beyond the prize to what would come next. The experience of racing around the world, immersing in different cultures, overcoming seemingly impossible challenges—it had awakened something in me that money alone couldn't satisfy.

The weeks after filming concluded were surreal. We returned to our regular lives, sworn to absolute secrecy about the outcome of the race. The show wouldn't air for months, and until then, no one could know we'd won. We both went back to our normal lives, carrying both the secret of our victory and questions about my next steps.

When *The Amazing Race* finally aired months later and Chris and I could publicly celebrate our victory, the immediate aftermath brought a flurry of local media attention, congratulatory messages from friends we hadn't heard from in years, and plenty of unsolicited advice about what to do with the money.

Through it all, I maintained my focus on the next step. While the show was airing, I had packed up my life again and moved to LA—this time with the mindset that I would do what those producers on *The Amazing Race* did for jobs. The day after the finale aired, I called Lynne from CBS—the one who rejected me from *Survivor* and then cast me on

*Amazing Race*. She was one of two people working in Hollywood whose phone numbers I had.

"Lynne, I've moved to LA. I'm looking for a job in TV. I'll take anything." In my mind, though, I really wanted a travel show.

"Good. My colleague Elizabeth is casting a new dating show called *Blind Date*. It's entry-level—basically a casting assistant position—but it would get your foot in the door."

Lynne got me the meeting, and I got the job. My first job in Hollywood!

That entry-level position wasn't glamorous work, but it provided crucial education in how television was actually created from the ground up. I was learning the rhythms of production, understanding the complex ecosystem of studios and production companies, building relationships, and proving myself through hard work rather than resting on the novelty of being a reality show winner.

The work itself was largely meeting people. My job was to go out and find good people to be on the show. How? Well, that was on me to figure out. Then I was screening applicants, scheduling interviews, handling paperwork—but I absorbed everything I could about development, production, post-production, and the business considerations that shaped creative decisions. During lunch breaks and after work, I built relationships with colleagues across different departments, asking questions and offering help wherever possible.

"Most people burn out within five years," a veteran producer named Frank Pace told me over coffee one day. "They come with stars in their eyes, thinking they'll create the next hit show immediately. When reality sets in—the long hours, the grunt work, the rejection—they can't handle it."

"What about the ones who make it?" I asked.

He considered this. "They're genuinely passionate about the process, not just the results. They're problem-solvers who thrive under pressure. And they build real relationships instead of just networking for advantage."

His description resonated with what I'd learned about myself through all my previous experiences. I genuinely loved the process of creating something meaningful, thrived when facing challenges without clear solutions, and valued authentic connections above transactional ones.

*The Amazing Race* prize money provided a buffer that many industry newcomers lacked—I could focus on learning and growing without the immediate pressure of paying rent.

But in every other way, I was starting from square one—learning the rhythms of production, understanding the complex ecosystem of studios and production companies, building relationships, and proving myself through hard work rather than resting on the novelty of being a reality show winner.

The real prize of *The Amazing Race* wasn't just the money, though that certainly changed my financial reality overnight. The real prize was clarity—a vivid glimpse of a path forward that combined my authentic strengths with meaningful work I felt called to do.

Some people race their entire lives without finding that kind of victory. I consider myself extraordinarily fortunate to have discovered it while literally racing around the world.

"Never get the big head."

# 13

# FROM SWEEPING FLOORS TO HOSTING SHOWS

Hollywood has a way of making you feel simultaneously special and completely insignificant. One minute you're a reality show winner with a modest level of fame; the next, you're just another aspiring producer in a city full of them. I'd been in Los Angeles for about a year, working my way up as a casting assistant to casting coordinator on "Blind Date," learning the industry from the inside out.

The work was interesting, if not exactly aligned with my ultimate goals. I was building skills, making connections, and paying my dues—all while my half-million-dollar cushion allowed me to focus on growth rather than mere survival. But I hadn't yet found my true entry point into the travel and adventure content I ultimately wanted to create.

Then came a series of calls that reminded me success doesn't always come from where you expect it.

A call came from Jacksonville—a city that had played a pivotal role in my journey through college and my brief return for graduate school. "Alex Boylan?" The voice on the phone was unfamiliar. "This is Kristi from PineRidge Film & Television in Jacksonville. We're developing a new adventure travel show called 'Dare USA,' and your name came up."

PineRidge Film & Television wasn't a household name, but in the industry, they had a solid reputation for creating quality travel and lifestyle content, particularly for networks like the Travel Channel and Discovery. They were headquartered not in Los Angeles or New York, but in Jacksonville, Florida—a city I had genuine connections to.

"We'd love to meet," Kristi continued. "If you're interested, we'd like you to come to Jacksonville to discuss potentially hosting."

This wasn't just another opportunity. This sounds almost too good to be true. It was specifically in the adventure travel space I wanted to be part of. But it would mean leaving Los Angeles just as I was establishing myself, trading the entertainment capital for a production company in Florida.

They asked when could I meet. I said as soon as they wanted. I made travel plans. Even though it didn't make sense, I felt a calling to this opportunity. I packed my bags and literally drove across the country for this meeting, sure that I was going to host a travel show.

## Jerry Smith and the Floor-Sweeping Offer

Arriving at their offices was a revelation. Unlike the sterile corporate spaces I'd become accustomed to in Los Angeles, PineRidge had created a vibrant, creative environment. The walls were adorned with memorabilia from their productions, editing suites hummed with activity, and at the center of it all was a vintage diner—literally a full-size diner inside their offices named *Jerry's Diner* after the owner, Jerry Smith—where the creative team gathered to brainstorm.

I was ushered in to meet Jerry Smith, the founder and creative force behind PineRidge. Silver-haired but with more energy than a 20-year-old, Jerry had built the company from scratch, developing a reputation for creating Emmy Award-winning authentic hit travel shows with talent that weren't star names.

"So you're *the Amazing Race* kid," he said, studying me with shrewd eyes. "Kristi speaks highly of you. Says you've got something special."

We talked for hours—not just about "Dare USA" and my potential role, but about our shared philosophies on travel, storytelling, and creating content that genuinely connected with audiences. Jerry made Samantha Brown into a star with his Travel Channel series *Great Hotels*, created award-winning documentaries, and built a very successful company outside the traditional entertainment hubs.

"Here's the situation," Jerry finally explained. "We're pitching 'Dare USA' to the network in a few weeks. The concept is solid, but we're still assembling the team. We think you could be a good fit as a host, but we need to see if the network likes the show and if they like you as a host."

I appreciated his honesty. This wasn't a job offer; it was an exploration of possibility. The project itself sounded perfect—an adventure travel show that would challenge participants to step outside their comfort zones in destinations across America. It aligned perfectly with my adventurous spirit and wanting any "in" I could to a travel show.

"I'd love to be part of the pitch," I told him. "What do you need from me?"

The next week was a whirlwind of preparation—developing presentation materials, refining the show concept, and practicing our pitch. I worked closely with the PineRidge, gaining insights into how shows were developed and sold that I hadn't been exposed to in my casting roles in LA.

Then came the pitch meeting with network executives. I'd been on the periphery of such meetings in Los Angeles but never at the center. Now I was part of the core team presenting "Dare USA" to decision-makers who could green-light the project.

The pitch went well—the executives asked engaged questions, seemed to connect with the concept, and responded positively to my potential involvement as host. As we left the meeting, the energy was high. Jerry seemed confident, Kristi was optimistic, and I felt I'd found a potential home for my ambitions in travel content.

Two weeks later, the call came. The network had decided not to move forward with "Dare USA."

It was a gut punch. The project that had seemed so promising, that had aligned so perfectly with my goals, that had brought me back to Jacksonville—gone in a single decision. This was the reality of the entertainment industry: most pitches never become shows, regardless of their quality or the passion behind them.

Disheartened by *The Travel Channel's* decision, I walked into Jerry's office. "Jerry," I said. "I want to work here. What would it take for me to get a job? I'll be honest—I believe in what you're doing. I'd sweep your floors if it meant me coming to work here every day."

There was a pause. "Sweep our floors, huh?" I could hear the smile in his voice.

Jerry went on to offer me a commission-only position selling stock footage to news stations—nothing glamorous, but a way into the company. PineRidge had an extensive library of footage that they licensed to news stations and production companies. My job would be to sell annual subscriptions to this service.

It wasn't hosting. It wasn't producing. It wasn't creative in any conventional sense. But it was a door into a company creating exactly the kind of content I wanted to be part of.

I started work immediately.

Leaving Los Angeles felt counterintuitive to many in my network there. I'd spent a year building connections, learning the industry, and establishing myself. Why abandon that progress for a commission-only sales position at a production company located in Jacksonville Florida?

But instinct told me this was the right move. PineRidge wasn't just any production company; they were specialists in travel content with a founder whose vision was infectious. And sometimes the direct path isn't the fastest route to your destination.

## The Real Education Begins

My first day at PineRidge was humbling in the best possible way. I was shown to a small desk in the back office, given a list of potential clients, and tasked with selling stock footage subscriptions by phone and fax. No glamour, no creative input, no connection to the travel shows being produced just rooms away.

My desk was about as far from glamorous as you could get—a small workspace in the back office, surrounded by shelves of archived footage, with a phone, a fax machine, and a computer running database software that looked like it belonged in the 1990s. This was command central for my stock footage sales operation, and I attacked it with the same determination I'd brought to selling calendars for my Brazil trip years earlier.

The stock footage library was PineRidge's bread and butter—a vast collection of video from their various productions that news stations and production companies could license for their own use. My job was straightforward: sell annual subscription packages that gave clients access to this footage, primarily to local TV stations across the country.

"It's not complicated," Jerry had explained during my brief training. "These stations need B-roll for their news and features. Weather footage, city scenes, lifestyle shots. Our library has high-quality material that they can't easily shoot themselves."

The work itself was unglamorous. Each morning, I'd arrive early, review my call list, and start dialing. Cold calling news directors and production managers, explaining PineRidge stock footage offerings, negotiating subscription rates, and following up on leads. Between calls, I'd prepare demo reels to showcase relevant footage and fax contracts to interested clients.

It was essentially a sales job, far removed from the creative aspects of production I ultimately wanted to be part of. But I approached it with genuine enthusiasm, not just as a means to an end but as an opportunity to understand the business from a different angle. I was genuinely excited to come to PineRidge every day. Even though I wasn't doing anything creative, I felt like part of the team and the energy all the producers had for the shows.

What surprised me was how much I learned from this seemingly peripheral role. Each conversation with a news director or producer revealed something about their content needs, budget constraints, and decision-making processes. I began to understand the economics of regional television in ways I never had in Los Angeles, where the focus was primarily on national networks and mainstream cable channels.

I also gained intimate knowledge of PineRidge's footage library—thousands of hours of travel, lifestyle, and cultural content from around the world. Searching for specific clips to meet client requests gave me a crash course in what made for usable, versatile footage. I began to recognize the difference between standard tourist shots and the more authentic, story-driven material that set PineRidge apart.

Despite the commission-only arrangement, I was doing well financially. My sales numbers consistently exceeded targets, partly due to genuine persistence and partly because I wasn't selling just for the commission—I was building relationships I hoped would serve me in my broader career goals.

But the real value wasn't in the commissions. It was in what happened between sales calls and after hours.

True to his word, Jerry began including me in creative meetings for ongoing and developing projects. At first, I mostly listened, absorbing the language and logic of development, understanding how ideas were refined, budgets constructed, and production challenges anticipated.

As I proved my worth, Jerry invited me to more active participation. "What do you think about this approach, Alex?" he'd ask during brainstorming sessions. Or, "You've been to Brazil—how would this concept work there?" My international experience and perspective as a former Amazing Race contestant gave me unique insights that the team found valuable.

Beyond the formal meetings, I spent every available moment learning from the various departments at PineRidge. When the sales phone wasn't ringing, I'd wander over to the edit bays, where Zsolt Luka and other editors were shaping raw footage into compelling stories.

"You're going to wear out your welcome," Zsolt joked the third time I appeared at his door. But he didn't send me away. Instead, he began explaining his process—how he selected moments that advanced the story, techniques for pacing that kept viewers engaged, and methods for creating emotional resonance through the juxtaposition of images, music, and dialogue.

"Editing isn't just technical," he told me. "It's storytelling. You're making a thousand tiny decisions that collectively determine whether viewers care about what they're watching."

I absorbed these lessons hungrily, recognizing their value far beyond traditional editing. Understanding how a story is constructed in post-production influenced how I thought about development, how I imagined scenes would play out, and learned how the entire production process worked. As they say, it all ends up in the edit bay.

On weekends and evenings, I volunteered as a production assistant on any shoot that would have me. This meant carrying equipment, managing release forms, handling basic lighting setups, and generally making myself useful in whatever way the production needed.

These experiences provided practical knowledge no film school could match. I learned the rhythms of production, the language of set operations, the hierarchy of roles, and the thousand small details that could make a shoot succeed or fail. I witnessed how producers and directors worked with subjects to capture authentic moments, how technical issues were resolved on the fly, and how the vision established in development translated (or sometimes failed to translate) into actual filming.

During one particularly grueling shoot for a lifestyle segment—sixteen hours in the Florida summer heat—the producer pulled me aside. "You know, most people with half a million dollars in the bank aren't out here sweating and hauling gear for no pay."

I laughed. "Maybe that's why I still have most of that half million. I'm investing in learning, not spending on lifestyle."

It was true. While *The Amazing Race* prize provided financial security, I was living modestly and focusing on building skills and relationships rather than projecting success. My house was comfortable but not flashy. My car was reliable, but nothing fancy. My wardrobe consisted mostly of casual clothes appropriate for production work.

This approach raised eyebrows among some colleagues who knew about my reality TV win, but it earned respect from the veterans at PineRidge who had built careers through substance rather than show.

Jerry, in particular, seemed to appreciate my methodology. About eight months into my time at PineRidge, he invited me to lunch at his office's vintage diner that served as the company's creative hub.

"You're doing good work with the footage sales," he acknowledged as we sat down. "But that's not why I wanted to talk. I've been watching how you've immersed yourself in every aspect of our operation. That's rare, especially for someone who started in front of the camera on such a big show as *The Amazing Race*."

He proceeded to offer me a more formal role in production, not replacing my sales position immediately, but adding responsibilities that would move me closer to my goal of creating travel content.

"We're developing a new show called *At The Chef's Table* for PBS," he said. "It explores the relationships between chef, restaurant, and the dining experience inside the kitchen doors. We think you would be a good host.

The show will have three segments—exploring with the chef about where they get their food, the food block making the meal, and then the celebration with famous people from that city eating with the chef and you at *At the Chef's Table* in the kitchen. We want to juxtapose this snooty life of high restaurants with a regular guy like 'you' exploring it."

It was the opportunity I'd been hoping for—a chance to step from behind the scenes into an on-camera role with a show that combined culinary exploration with human connection. The screen test went well, and to my amazement, Jerry offered me the hosting position.

"You're not the obvious choice," he explained frankly. "We could get someone with more hosting experience or culinary credentials. But you bring something different—an authentic curiosity and ability to connect with people that can't be taught."

I'll never forget that first shoot. I was on a shrimp boat in Amelia Island, Florida. It felt like 200 degrees out. On top of that, I was a nervous wreck. I looked at all the production people—the amount of time, energy, and money that had gotten the production here. And I was about to do my first on-camera. I couldn't stop sweating from both the heat and the nerves. How did I get here? Am I a con artist (something Jerry asked me if I felt years later—he said it's common, and sometimes even he feels like one)?

Soon enough, I was so sweaty they couldn't shoot. They had to put dryer sheets on my chest under my clothes to control it. I wanted to run away. Maybe this wasn't for me. But I kept thinking of all the hard things I did and just kept saying to myself, "Stay in the game, Alex"—a mantra I tell young people now. Half the job is just staying in the game until you are the only one left.

But soon enough, to my surprise, *At the Chef's Table*, the ratings were the highest on PBS at the time, becoming the highest-rated food show on the network during its run. Suddenly, I found myself not just hosting but also producing, leveraging everything I'd learned during my unglamorous beginnings at PineRidge.

What made this success especially meaningful wasn't just the creative fulfillment or professional advancement. It was knowing I'd earned it through humility, persistence, and a willingness to start at the bottom—literally offering to sweep floors if necessary.

Jerry became not just a boss but a mentor and a second father figure, sharing wisdom accumulated through decades in the industry. He had a way of keeping me grounded even as opportunities expanded. "Success is temporary," he'd say, "but the work ethic that creates it should be permanent. And *never* get the big head, Alex—that is everyone's downfall in this business."

This is something Jerry says to me even to this day at 86 years old.

This philosophy resonated deeply with my own experience—that the most valuable opportunities often come disguised as humble beginnings or apparent setbacks. My journey from Brazil to Germany to Boston to St. John to *The Amazing Race* had taught me that lesson repeatedly. Now, my path from Los Angeles to a back-office sales position to hosting and producing reinforced it once more.

The irony wasn't lost on me: I'd had to leave the entertainment capital to find my true entry point into the roles and responsibilities I was hoping to get in the entertainment business. I'd had to step away from the prestige of my Los Angeles connections to find a mentor who would give me real opportunities to grow.

Most importantly, I'd had to be willing to start at the bottom again—even with half a million dollars in the bank and a reality TV win on my resume—because I understood that genuine opportunity comes to those who value learning and listening over status.

As *At the Chef's Table* gained traction and my role at PineRidge expanded to include both hosting and producing responsibilities, I reflected on the circuitous route that had brought me here. If I hadn't attended Jacksonville University, I might never have developed connections to this city. If I hadn't won *The Amazing Race*, I might not have had the financial freedom to take a commission-only job while pursuing my true goals. If the "Dare USA" pitch hadn't failed, I might never have joined PineRidge the way I did and discovered the mentor who would shape my understanding to how to navigate and thrive in the tough business of television.

Each apparent detour had been an essential part of the journey. Each "no" had ultimately led to a more meaningful "yes." The path hadn't been direct or predictable, but it had led exactly where I needed to go.

And it had all started with a willingness to sweep the floors—to begin at the beginning, not out of necessity but out of genuine passion for the work itself. That humility, I was learning, wasn't a detour from success but a prerequisite for it.

The lesson wasn't just about career strategy; it was about a fundamental approach to life. True opportunity doesn't always arrive in expected packaging or follow conventional paths. Sometimes it begins with a failed pitch, a back-office desk, and a simple statement: "I'll sweep your floors if it means being part of what you're producing."

Throughout this period, Jerry continued as a crucial mentor, pushing me to expand my capabilities while keeping my ego in check. "You're doing well," he would say when a show received positive reviews or strong ratings, "but never forget there are a thousand people who could do your job. What makes you valuable isn't your face on camera—it's your understanding of the whole process."

This humbling perspective kept me hungry to learn more, to contribute beyond my official responsibilities, and to understand aspects of production outside my immediate focus. When not filming my own shows, I'd shadow directors on other PineRidge projects, sit in on development meetings for shows I wasn't involved with, and volunteer for challenging shoots that would expand my experience.

About four years into my time at PineRidge, with both *At the Chef's Table* and *Animal Attractions* established as successful series, Jerry invited me to lunch in his diner, typically ordering Bono's BBQ, a local staple in Jacksonville at the time. These meetings had become something of a tradition—opportunities for more philosophical discussions about career and content beyond the day-to-day operations.

"You've grown a lot," he observed as we settled into a booth. "From selling stock footage to hosting and producing two successful shows. What's next? What do you really want to create?"

It was a question I'd been considering myself. While I found genuine fulfillment in my current roles, I'd begun imagining a project that would combine elements of everything I'd experienced—from my exchange year in Brazil to *The Amazing Race* to my current work creating travel series.

"I want to create something that challenges how people think about travel," I told him. "Not just showing beautiful destinations or tourist experiences, but demonstrating how stepping outside your comfort zone in unfamiliar environments can transform you."

Jerry nodded encouragingly. "Keep going."

"I'm thinking about a show that puts the viewer in the position I was in during *The Amazing Race*—navigating unfamiliar places, connecting with locals across cultural barriers, solving problems with limited resources. But without the artificial competition element. Real travel. Real people, Real stories."

"Sounds ambitious," Jerry said. "But potentially powerful. What's holding you back from developing it?"

His question cut to the heart of something I'd been reluctant to acknowledge. Despite my growth at PineRidge and Jerry's generous mentorship, I was beginning to feel the pull toward creating something that was wholly mine, not just hosting or producing within an established company, but building a project from the ground up with my own vision.

"I guess I'm trying to figure out if it's something I should develop here at PineRidge or..." I hesitated.

"Or if it's time for you to spread your wings," Jerry finished for me. "That's a fair question."

His response surprised me. I'd expected encouragement to keep building my career at PineRidge, not acknowledgment that I might be ready for something more independent.

"Look," he continued, "I didn't build PineRidge to keep talent trapped here forever. I built it to create great content and help people grow. Sometimes that growth eventually takes them beyond our walls."

His generosity of spirit was humbling. Here was a successful company founder encouraging me to consider my own path forward, even if it might eventually lead away from his organization.

"I'm not saying it's time to go," Jerry clarified. "You've still got plenty to learn here, and we value what you bring to our projects. But it's healthy to be thinking about your unique contribution to this industry."

That conversation planted a seed that would gradually grow into my next major endeavor. While continuing my work on *Animal Attractions* and a few other series, I began developing concepts for what would eventually become *Around the World for Free*—a groundbreaking interactive travel series that would combine everything I'd learned from *The Amazing Race*, PineRidge, and my earlier travels.

As I prepared to transform this concept from idea to reality, I carried with me Jerry's constant reminder: "Never get the big head." The stock footage salesman willing to sweep floors had become a host-producer of a successful series, but the fundamental values remained unchanged—humility that enables continuous learning, authentic connection that creates genuine relationships, and work ethic that proves commitment beyond words.

The journey from that back-office desk with its phone and fax machine to developing and hosting shows that reached national audiences hadn't been quick or direct. It had involved countless cold calls, endless questions, weekend shoots without compensation, and a willingness to learn aspects of production that initially seemed far removed from my goals.

But looking back, I wouldn't have changed a single step. Each phase—even the unglamorous ones, perhaps especially those—had contributed something essential to my development as a producer and content creator. The back office where I'd sold stock footage had provided a more valuable education than any executive suite could have offered. Sometimes the most important rooms in building a career aren't the ones with the best views or the most prestigious titles. They're the ones that show you how things actually work, from the foundation up.

> "Each step is built upon the previous one, creating a foundation of skills and perspectives."

# 14

# "COULD YOU DO IT FOR FREE?"

Ideas rarely arrive fully formed. They evolve from fragments, from questions, from passing comments that lodge in your mind and refuse to leave. The concept that would become *Around the World for Free* began with an interesting experience and a simple remark at a post-screening event for *At the Chef's Table*.

## When Disasters Become Discoveries

During my time living back in Jacksonville and working at PineRidge, myself and three close friends—Dov, Ben and Fab—were doing a lot of surf trips to Central America. Still in the early days of cell phones and the internet, our travels were as raw as it gets. We would just buy our plane tickets to a country where we had 'heard' there were good waves. Get off the plane, rent a car and just explore the coastline looking for waves. Costa Rica, Panama, Nicaragua…every chance we got we would all get together and go searching for waves.

During this time, we started to bring a little handy camera along filming our adventures. We would have friends edit some fun videos. And eventually we made an official DVD…Dropping In…Panama was the first one. It was pretty raw, but the journey of actually filming, editing, making the DVD cover art and calling Surf Shops to try and get them to buy it was a real joy for me. I enjoyed the process. This was getting my feet wet with doing my own production without really thinking too much about it. I loved traveling with my buddies, the unknown of trying to find a hidden surf break, and the entire business of trying to capture and sell this to an audience via DVD and surf shops. Dropping In…Panama was mildly successful at best.

## THE MILES THAT MAKE YOU

At PineRidge, Zsolt and I had become close friends. And while we were talking about doing the next iteration Dropping In…El Salvador I mentioned to Zsolt…could we hire you to edit it and spruce up the production value. Once again, Zsolt Luka is an Emmy nominated editor and I almost felt embarrassed asking him. His response: 'I'll edit if I can direct.' I was like hell yea brotha.

So we planned the trip, and now, with Zsolt (a real pro), we set off to make *Dropping In…El Salvador*. Back then, El Salvador was pretty rough—lots of poverty, gang violence, etc., that we needed to navigate. So I called the tourism board and they highly suggested we have security at all times while filming in the country. They lined us up with some and we were on our way. El Salvador has a strip of 8 right hand point breaks all within a 50-mile stretch, each mimicking what can rarely be found in the USA outside of Malibu. It was epic.

But about one week into filming all hell broke loose with a hurricane hitting shore, volcano erupting, mud slides, you name it. The government pulled our security and we were holed up in the seaside town of La Libertad. While letting the time pass we played cards, drank beers and pretty much did nothing. But everyone kept telling us not to go up into the favelas.

Behind our hotel was a hillside favela—a little town built into the side of a hill. These are common across Latin America. All the locals implored us not to go up there. They said it was dangerous for tourists like us and that we would 'die'; if we went up there. Zsolt and I would laugh, what, they are going to literally kill us for going up there. So we made a pack. Once the hurricane passed we would attempt together to make it to the top of the favela without dying. It couldn't be that dangerous, right? At the last minute Zsolt grabbed a camera and said 'you walk first and i'll film you. That way, if we die, at least it is recorded. So we decided to bring the camera and see what happens.

Sure enough, locals popped out of their makeshift homes to see what these two gringos were doing. They'd see the camera, then get excited—"Hola amigo!" they'd say. "Vamos!" They ushered us into their homes with the camera rolling. They wanted to show us how they lived. They were using garbage cans as ovens. They were housing up to 10 people in one small room. They would cook together, and then they started cooking (what little food they had left) for us. They had barely anything to eat, but they shared everything they had with Zsolt and me.

It was fascinating. Needless to say, we were glad we went up there. We came down from the mountain, already talking about how this experience might become a show concept on its own—exploring nooks and crannies all over the world, seeing and experiencing how people live all over the world. The idea for *Around the World for Free* was percolating…

Zsolt and I knew we captured something pretty awesome. And I couldn't get the idea out of my head. Once home from the surf trip I made Dropping In…El Salvador with Zsolt working nights and weekends. But both of us were more interested in the footage we captured going up the mountain than the surf documentary itself.

Back in Jacksonville, I attended an event with some producers. Someone casually asked me about doing (hypothetically) a travel show. "You won *The Amazing Race*," they said. "It would be easy for you to travel the world!"

I smiled politely, but the comment stuck with me. There was a fundamental misunderstanding in his assumption that my background gave me special access to travel experiences unavailable to others. The truth was quite different. Growing up on the North Shore of Boston with limited means, I'd sold calendars door-to-door to fund my exchange year in Brazil. I'd navigated my way to the island of St. John with no map and a few hundred dollars left on my credit card. My most meaningful travel experiences hadn't been about luxury or privilege but about connecting with people across cultural and economic divides. But it's hard for people who don't know you to understand the road I had traveled to get there.

On the drive home that evening, I kept returning to that comment. "It's easy for you to travel." What if I could prove the opposite? What if I could demonstrate that meaningful travel wasn't about money or special access but about openness, human connection, and a willingness to step outside your comfort zone?

## From Criticism to Creation

The kernel of an idea began forming: What if I traveled around the world with no money at all? Not just on a budget, but with literally zero dollars, relying entirely on the kindness of strangers, work exchanges, and the human connections that make travel transformative? Could you do it for free?

It was an audacious concept, perhaps even foolhardy. But it resonated with everything I believed about travel and human connection. It also aligned with my growing interest in creating content that wasn't just entertaining but potentially life-changing for viewers.

The next morning, I told Zsolt Luka about the off-handed comment. I walked him through the concept of what if we did it with no money.

"That's not just a travel show," he said. "That's a human experiment. And I'm in brotha."

Zsolt and I had been collaborating on side projects beyond our PineRidge responsibilities—mostly surf documentaries and short travel pieces we created on weekends and during vacation time. These projects allowed us to experiment with different storytelling approaches without the constraints of network expectations or formal production structures.

I took the concept to Jerry at PineRidge, showing him our El Salvador footage and outlining the expanded vision for *Around the World for Free*. His response was measured but encouraging.

"It's ambitious," he acknowledged. "Maybe too ambitious for PineRidge right now. This is breaking new ground in terms of production model, distribution, and audience engagement. But I think it's worth pursuing."

His candid assessment was both disappointing and liberating. I had hoped PineRidge might produce the project, leveraging the company's resources and expertise. But I also recognized that the concept might require a different approach—one that would allow for greater experimentation and risk than an established production company could reasonably accommodate.

"So what's your advice?" I asked Jerry.

"Take it to LA," he said simply. "PineRidge has given you a solid foundation in traditional production. But what you're describing goes beyond traditional. You need to connect with people who are thinking about the future of media, not just current formats."

## "COULD YOU DO IT FOR FREE?"

It was a pivotal moment—Jerry essentially giving me permission to pursue my vision beyond PineRidge walls. Not because he didn't believe in the concept, but because he recognized it might require resources and connections that PineRidge couldn't provide.

"This doesn't mean you're leaving PineRidge permanently," he clarified. "Your shows here are successful, and that door remains open. But this particular project might need a different approach."

With Jerry's blessing, I began planning my move back to Los Angeles to explore potential partnerships for *Around the World for Free*.

So I got in my car (again) with all my belongings and drove back to LA with this idea of *Around the World for Free*. I moved back in with my little sister Alexis, who was out in LA pursuing her acting career. By this time, Reality TV had really taken off and CBS was the king—*Survivor*, *Big Brother*, etc. And many of the contestants had made their way to LA. We had an awesome little community of ex-reality stars. Thursday - Sunday, you could find us all in Hollywood bouncing from Katana, Saddle Ranch, The Sky Bar, and Barny's Beanery

Enter Burton Roberts, a fellow reality TV alum from *Survivor: Pearl Islands*. One night over some tequila at Barney's Beanery, Burton and I started talking about the transition from contestant to producer. Burton and I had similar paths—both corporate guys who hated that world and found our way to producing. Burton was one of the few who actually turned nothing into something. He had an idea of taking reality TV stars up to Big Bear and filming it. He sold it to Fox Reality. One evening, while exchanging Tequila shots, we decided we should be working together. The next day, I came to his place and we started talking things over. *Around the World for Free* kept making its way to the top, and we said, 'let's do it'. It was as simple as that. We've been business partners ever since.

Our first conversation revealed an immediate synergy in our thinking. Burton brought complementary skills—a background in business development and technology that balanced my production experience and on-camera capabilities. He also shared my vision of creating content that went beyond entertainment to potentially transform how people engaged with the world.

"The interactive component is key," Burton emphasized during one of our planning sessions. "This can't just be a show about traveling without money. It needs to be a platform where viewers become participants—suggesting routes, offering connections, even providing shelter or meals if you pass through their area."

Together, we refined the concept further, always calling up Zsolt when we had another breakthrough with the idea to make sure he felt good about it. We were developing a production model that would require minimal crew—just me as host-traveler and a single camera operator/editor (Zsolt) who would document the journey. No producers on the ground, no fixers arranging experiences in advance, no safety net beyond what we could create through human connections and interactive audience engagement.

With the concept clarified and Burton as a partner, my return to Los Angeles with renewed purpose was feeling great. Burton and I pitched this show all over Los Angeles to anyone who would take a meeting.

"Love the concept" became a familiar refrain, followed inevitably by, "but we don't have a framework for this kind of project."

The traditional TV networks couldn't envision how to package and distribute an interactive journey without a predetermined structure. There were no digital platforms at the time. Facebook and YouTube were barely a thing. So the main networks were intrigued by the interactive elements but questioned whether production quality could be maintained while traveling without money or traditional crew support.

After what felt like a hundred meetings and multiple promising but ultimately unsuccessful discussions, Burton and I faced a crossroads. We believed deeply in the concept's potential, but the conventional paths to production seemed closed to such an unconventional project.

"Maybe we're thinking too conventionally about an unconventional idea," Burton suggested during a particularly discouraging moment. "Let's stop trying to fit this into existing production models and create our own."

That shift in thinking—from seeking approval within established systems to creating an entirely new approach—would prove transformative. If existing production companies couldn't accommodate our vision, we would become the production company. If networks weren't ready for this interactive model, we would build direct relationships with audiences

## "COULD YOU DO IT FOR FREE?"

through the platform we would create. So we pooled our resources to fund the production ourselves.

During this development period, I maintained my responsibilities at PineRidge, flying between Jacksonville and Los Angeles to balance existing commitments with this new venture. Jerry continued his support, adjusting my schedule to accommodate this exploration while encouraging me to maintain the foundation I'd built at PineRidge.

"Don't burn bridges while building new ones," he advised when I expressed concern about dividing my focus. "What you're creating might become something extraordinary, or it might teach you valuable lessons that bring a new perspective to your work here. Either outcome is worthwhile."

His wisdom exemplified what made Jerry such an extraordinary mentor—the ability to support growth even when it might ultimately lead beyond his company, coupled with practical advice about maintaining professional relationships throughout transitions.

Burton and I kept hearing no after no after no.

Burton and I continued to refine the concept, testing interactive elements and building potential distribution strategies. Then a surprising source of validation emerged. Ghen Maynard took a second meeting with us. He was credited with pushing *Survivor* and *Amazing Race* through at CBS. He was a big deal at the network. After Ghen turned us down for the second time, he wrote me an email. "Alex, this reminds me of when I was pushing to get *Survivor* on air," he wrote. "Many people told me no, and it couldn't be done. So even though this is a pass from CBS, I want to say I like what you and Burton are trying to do."

Despite the no, that email felt like a win. Everyone was intrigued by the pitches, and that gave us confidence. And over time, the project kept evolving more and more into a multi-platform daily interactive experience that would leverage emerging digital capabilities to create new relationships between content creators and audiences. The journey itself would remain central, but the surrounding ecosystem of interaction, contribution, and community would transform it from passive viewing into active participation.

This evolution aligned perfectly with my own journey from reality contestant to stock footage salesman to host-producer. Each step had built upon the previous one, creating a foundation of skills and perspectives that prepared me for this unconventional venture. The calendar sales that funded my Brazil exchange, *the Amazing Race* experience, and the humble beginning at PineRidge—all had contributed to both the concept and my readiness to pursue it.

As our development progressed, Burton and I recognized that launching *Around the World for Free* would require a leap of faith—a commitment to begin the journey without all elements secured in advance. Much like traveling without money would require trusting in human connection and improvisation, producing the project would demand similar faith in the concept's ability to generate its own momentum.

One week, Burton and I flew to New York City to meet with a few networks about the concept. While we were still as excited as ever, we still hadn't hit our first big win. On a snowy afternoon, we met with Anne O'Grady—she ran CBS's marketing for decades and had been a big player behind the network's reality TV success. Hilariously, Burton and I went to three of the wrong CBS buildings before eventually finding Anne's office. By the time we arrived, we looked like a disaster. We were soaked with snow and even sweating from all the walking. And we were super late.

"Guys, I almost left," Anne said. That was understandable. It was Friday evening, almost 6 pm. You could tell she was a bit annoyed.

Nevertheless, she ushered us into her office and we immediately started pitching *Around the World for Free.*

"Are you really pitching me a show concept right now?" Anne said. Now she was even more annoyed. "I run marketing here. I can't take a pitch. I'm not the person you want to talk to. You need to go back to Los Angeles and talk to Ghen."

We explained that we'd already met twice with Ghen. He'd said no both times. Before she could respond, I pulled out a DVD with our trailer on it. Anne smiled and said 'let's have a watch'.

After a minute, Anne perked up. "Why isn't CBS doing this!?! Tell me what you guys need." From there, we discussed details. We didn't

## "COULD YOU DO IT FOR FREE?"

want money or anything like that. We simply wanted to know if *The Early Show* would follow us. Anne wasn't sure, but she set us up a meeting.

A week later, Anne, Burton, and I met with *The Early Show* executive producer in New York. This was their famous daily lifestyle news program that ran from 1999 to 2012. He was smoking a cigar and seemed only mildly interested in us. But everyone at the network loved Anne and you could tell he was doing a favor for her. Anne thanked him for the meeting, then turned it over to us. We did our dog-and-pony show yet again, walking step-by-step through our interactive show concept. We explained why we thought *The Early Show* was the best place to launch this show live—by engaging with their daily audience, viewers could get a a recap once a week there and be pushed to our platform for daily content. It was perfect synergy.

When we finished our spiel, the cigar-smoking executive smiled and leaned back in his chair. He was silent for what felt like five whole minutes before speaking.

"Boys, there never was a stunt I didn't like. You've got *The Early Show*. Launch it here and we'll follow you."

We were thrilled. We thanked him and Anne with everything inside us, then flew back home to start planning.

We set a target date, developed a minimal production plan, and began building the interactive platform that would allow audience participation. The journey would begin in New York and circumnavigate the globe, before returning to the United States—all without me touching any money. Zsolt Luka would be filming and editing in real time, and together we would live, eat, and sleep with locals wherever the journey took us. This was a huge leap of faith for Zsolt—someone with multiple Emmy nominations—who committed to being the backbone for the production.

I called Jerry with the news.

"Thanks for stealing my best editor, Alex," he said jokingly. "It might work, it might fail," Jerry told me, "but you'll learn something valuable either way. And there's always a place for you here when you and Zsolt return."

As the departure date approached, the project that had begun with an unexpected travel experience and an offhand comment at a screening event was becoming a reality. We had minimal funding from me and Zsolt. Burton came in and said he would manage the business side, and for us not to worry. Let's go make this show, and I will handle the rest. So here we are with an experimental production model and an untested interactive platform. But we also had something more valuable—a concept that resonated deeply with fundamental truths about travel, human connection, and authentic experience.

The question that had sparked the idea—"Could you do it for free?"—was about to be answered. But the journey would reveal that "free" didn't mean without value or exchange. It meant freeing travel from the transactional mindset that often separated travelers from authentic cultural experiences. It meant creating free access for audiences to participate in a global journey. And personally, it meant freeing myself to create content aligned with my deepest values rather than fitting into established formats.

The path from that initial spark to launching *Around the World for Free* had been neither direct nor easy. It had required leaving the security of PineRidge support, forming new partnerships, and repeatedly facing rejection from traditional production channels. But each obstacle had refined the concept, strengthened our commitment, and clarified the project's unique potential.

As I packed my backpack for the journey—the same one that had accompanied me to Brazil, through Europe, to Germany, to St. John, and during *The Amazing Race*—I reflected on how this moment connected to everything that had come before. The blue-collar kid from Georgetown, Massachusssets, who sold calendars to fund his first international adventure was now preparing to circle the globe with no money, documenting the journey for an interactive audience experience.

The circle felt complete, yet also like the beginning of something entirely new. *Around the World for Free* wasn't just another production; it was the culmination of every lesson learned and every value developed throughout my journey—and the foundation for whatever would come next.

"Step beyond the boundaries of certainty into the realm where growth happens."

# 15

# 159 DAYS *AROUND THE WORLD FOR FREE*

Standing at CBS's outside plaza between East 58th and East 59th Streets, near the southeast corner of Central Park, surrounded by *The Early Show* cameras, producers with headsets, and curious onlookers, I felt a familiar mix of exhilaration and terror.

## Zero Dollars, Infinite Possibilities

But this time was different. During *The Amazing Race*, I had a partner, the structure of a competition, and a production team managing logistics behind the scenes. Now, I had just Zsoltt Luka behind the camera, a backpack containing minimal essentials, and exactly zero dollars to my name. No credit cards, no emergency cash, no pre-arranged accommodations or transportation. Just the clothes on my back, a passport, and a concept we believed in but had never fully tested.

We had built what was one of the first websites of its kind, almost like building a Facebook page before Facebook existed. The interactive platform AroundTheWorldForFree.com was designed to let viewers follow our journey in real-time and even help guide our path. But technology being what it was in those days, *The Early Show* appearance soon nearly crashed our website, making it hard to get messages through initially. Why did our website nearly crash?

*The Early Show* really blew us up. They teased the launch multiple times and conducted a full interview with me and Zsolt on the outside lot. Harry, the host at the time, really got behind the project, and his genuine interest and intrigue got the audience excited. He implored viewers to get involved, which many did! The segment culminated with us launching live right from the show before walking off set to begin our journey.

Then, with cameras rolling and Zsolt filming me walking off the set live, I stepped away from the security of the television studio and into the uncertainty of New York City with no money and a world to cross. The journey had officially begun.

**The First Act of Kindness**

Our first challenge emerged immediately: how to get out of Manhattan. Within thirty minutes of walking off the CBS set, our first message came through the sporadic website connection: "Hey, tickets are waiting for you to get to Florence, South Carolina. Love to house Alex and Zsolt, show you both around this area, and help you on your way."

We were sweating it out and I remember thinking, "Oh my gosh, this whole idea might work."

But first, we needed to get to Grand Central Station. We were walking through Manhattan when we passed a construction site, maybe four blocks from the CBS studio. I struck up a conversation with the construction workers, explaining what we were trying to do—make it around the world without money, and they were the first people I'd talked to.

One guy asked, "Where do you need to go?"

"We just got a train ticket to Florence, South Carolina," I replied.

"I'll give you a ride to the train station," he said.

Next thing we knew, we were in his truck as he drove us through Manhattan. This guy was a character—yelling, beeping his horn, making way through traffic, "Everyone in New York City knows me," he announced. "I'm known as the food bandit. Anyone who gets in my way, I chuck some nice Chinese food on their car." And he was literally throwing food out the window as we drove.

This one random person's random act of kindness set the tone for everything that would follow on *Around the World for Free*.

**Heading South Through the Americas**

We didn't have much of a plan except that winter was coming in September, so we decided to head south. We made our way down the East

Coast through South Carolina and Florida, eventually breaking international ground in Puerto Rico and making our way through the Caribbean.

In the Caribbean, we had some incredible experiences. On the island of Tortola, people mistook me for a motivational speaker and began bringing me around to different islands to address local kids. A Reverend had written in suggesting I visit, and before I knew it, I was being introduced to island communities as a motivational speaker.

I got literally stuck on the island of Dominica, way down in the Leeward Islands. It's an incredible place—they're still finding hundred-foot waterfalls, and it has the second-largest boiling lake in the world. But I got there and just couldn't get off the island for a while until someone helped arrange passage.

Eventually, we broke into South America through Caracas, Venezuela. This was during Hugo Chavez's presidency, so the country was deeply divided and torn. We stayed with two families who had written in with completely opposing perspectives. One family worked for the government and urged their fellow Venezuelans, "You should stay in Venezuela. Help the people of Venezuela stand up and make Venezuela right"—easy words when you're on the government payroll.

The other family owned several hair salons, and the father was trying to get his whole family out of the country because of the political unrest. So we were seeing two sides of what was happening in this fascinating, divided country.

Eventually, someone wrote in saying there was a bus ticket that would take us to Lima, Peru. This bus ride was supposed to take three days, but being a third-world bus—I'm talking chickens and everything—it ended up taking eight or nine days. Zsolt and I were on a bus from Caracas, Venezuela, through the mountains of Colombia, into Peru, and down to Lima.

This bus was breaking down every five seconds. So many people were trying to escape Venezuela at the time that we'd be hiding people in the bathrooms while crossing checkpoints. There was a point in Colombia where I was helping these two young girls sneak across the border—so many people were just trying to get out of the political unrest happening in Venezuela.

We had amazing experiences throughout South America, including Machu Picchu, but there was that time in the Atacama Desert where I was completely stranded. That was one of those "is this it?" moments—I'm in the middle of nowhere, really stuck.

Someone had written into our message board with just an address, saying, "If you can get here, you have a place to stay." I'd gotten a ride or was on a bus somewhere in the middle of nowhere when someone told me to get off. It was like three o'clock in the morning, and I don't speak Spanish that well. I got off in this little village in the middle of the Atacama Desert.

I found what I thought was the right house and started knocking on the door. No one was answering—it's three or four in the morning. Eventually, I heard someone, and this lady came down and walked me up to a bedroom where I just collapsed from exhaustion.

## The Big Ocean Jumps

One of the biggest challenges Zsolt, Burton, and I had talked about was how we would cross oceans prior to launching *Around the World for Free*. We never knew how that would happen. I thought I would work on cargo ships, but that takes longer and is harder than you think, given all the legal requirements.

In the midst of struggling to make it down the Chilean coastline through the Atacama Desert, someone had written in saying, "Hey, I've always wanted to go on a safari. Chances are, I'm never going to do it. Alex, there's a plane ticket waiting for you in Santiago, Chile. If you can make it to Santiago, there's a plane ticket that will take you across the ocean to South Africa." It was kind of fun—the first time I was given a mission. Someone had been super generous, but my mission was to go on a safari in honor of this person who wrote in.

We traveled up the East Coast of Africa—South Africa, Tanzania, Kenya. While in Kenya, we spent time with Maasai warriors. I was working with a Kenyan outfitter, basically working the campsites and helping out in order to stay with them.

But then we got back to Nairobi, and there was a change in the elections. When the election happened, all hell broke loose. I'd never seen anything like it—a country falling apart, mass violence. I was in downtown

Nairobi, surrounded by National Guard, as video footage shows, because the whole country of Kenya was just collapsing.

As you can imagine, CBS was like, "We have a guy out there," so I was doing more live hits with *The Early Show* as all this went down. It was a catastrophic situation. I could see beyond the city perimeter, just burning.

We visited Uhuru Park, a major park in Nairobi, accompanied by a local reporter. At this park you could see all the big networks like Sky News, CNN, and BBC. Zolt was filming me trying to tell our story to our audience. Someone from Sky News came over and asked, "Why are you smiling? " I was trying to explain that I'd somehow found myself in this war-torn country, which I never expected, and when I get uncomfortable, I smile.

Someone wrote in with a ticket to get out and get us to India. We tried to get passage to India, but because of the war breaking out, we didn't have proper visas. India thought we were lying and sent us back to Nairobi. Now we're living in an airport until someone from a news station who knew our story brings us into their home. It was mayhem for a while. But a great story for the audience to follow in real time.

## Southeast Asia Adventures

Eventually, we made it to Thailand, which was amazing. Buddhist culture. Beautiful beaches to the south, mountains to the north. We walked across the border into Cambodia, and the crossing from Thailand to Cambodia felt like stepping into a Mexican border town compared to America—dramatically different.

When we got into Cambodia, every dusty road felt like going back in time. Everyone was staring at these two white guys with a camera. Zsolt and I were a bit nervous as we were getting surrounded by people, so we just started walking down this dirt path. There were six huts with monks sitting in them, and one monk was essentially asking if we wanted to stay there. We lived with those monks in the border town of Cambodia for about a week. It was amazing. No travel series had ever captured this type of raw travel before.

Eventually, a missionary in Phnom Penh heard about our story and drove 8 hours to come out to pick us up. We made our way back to

Phnom Penh and told the story of Cambodia, which is rich in history but tough too, with the killing fields and Pol Pot's legacy.

We continued through Vietnam, where we were there for the Chinese New Year in the city of Natrang on the coast, which was just insane—one of the most incredible things ever. If you ever get a chance to go to Vietnam for Chinese New Year, do it.

Eventually, we got passage back to the States and crisscrossed America, which was almost like a celebration tour because everyone in the States knew about us by then. We were stopping at schools that had been following our journey.

There was a school in Minnesota where, when we arrived, they literally had every stop of our journey mapped on the walls. The teachers had been using *Around the World for Free* to teach their elementary and middle school kids about geography and travel. When the teacher wrote in saying they'd been following us and asking if we could come through, imagine how magical it was when we actually showed up.

Eventually, we wrapped it up back on *The Early Show*, completing the 159-day journey around the world without spending a dollar.

## The Legacy Continues

*Around the World for Free* demonstrated something profound: that meaningful travel and human connection don't require financial resources. They require authenticity, vulnerability, and a willingness to engage with the world and the people in it on their terms.

The interactive community that formed around our journey wasn't just following an adventure—they were actively creating it alongside us. From that first construction worker in Manhattan to the family in the Atacama Desert to the monks in Cambodia, every connection proved that people everywhere are fundamentally generous when given the opportunity to participate in something meaningful.

The journey validated our core premise: that the most valuable aspects of travel have everything to do with human connection and nothing to do with economic transaction. In 159 days, covering 4 continents, 16 countries spanning 45,000 miles without spending a dollar, we had created something entirely new—not just in travel content, but in the relationship between content creators and the audience.

And that foundation would become the launching pad for everything Around the World Productions would build next.

"Authentic human connection transcends cultural and economic boundaries."

# 16

# A NETWORK DEAL

Returning to normal life after 159 days of traveling without money was a surreal experience. Simple activities—buying coffee, taking a taxi, sleeping in the same bed for consecutive nights—felt strangely foreign after months of constant improvisation and reliance on human connection rather than financial transactions.

But there was little time to adjust. The momentum generated by *Around the World for Free* had created opportunities that demanded immediate attention. The interactive community remained engaged, the content we'd created needed organization and distribution, and media interest in the concept continued growing.

Burton and I established a small office out of a house rental in Santa Monica on the west side of Los Angeles to serve as headquarters for Around the World Productions. Unlike our pre-journey space filled with concept boards and pitch materials, this office buzzed with the energy of a successful project transitioning into a sustainable business. We hired a small team to manage the website, organize our massive content archive, and develop strategies for building on what we'd created.

A few days after wrapping up *Around the World for Free*, the phone calls started coming in. The executive producer of *The Rachael Ray Show*, Shane Farley, called. "We want to test the *Around the World for Free* concept, but here in the States for the Rachel Ray audience," Shane said he loved the interactive elements and authenticity—he thought this might resonate with Rachel's viewers. So, a similar concept called *Rach to the Rescue* emerged and entered pre-production. Needless to say, Burton and I were pumped. We were actually going to get paid 'in advance' for producing something.

Then Lori Rothchild called, a producer from *The Travel Channel*. They were building a concept of mapping the world with short-form videos. She wanted to know if we would be their production partner to produce this content. Another win!

## Ed Wilson's Vision: When the Right Executive Calls

But the biggest opportunity emerged from an unexpected source. Burton had been invited to speak at his alma mater, Southern Methodist University, about innovative media and entrepreneurship. During his presentation, he shared the story of *Around the World for Free*—how we'd developed the concept, faced rejection from traditional media channels, created our own production model, and built an engaged interactive community.

In the audience was Ed Wilson, a television executive who had recently taken leadership of WGN America, a cable network seeking to establish a distinct identity in an increasingly crowded media landscape. Wilson approached Burton after the presentation, intrigued by what he had heard.

"You've created something genuinely new," Wilson told him. "Not just a travel show, but a model for audience engagement that could transform how content is developed and distributed."

This conversation led to a meeting in Chicago with Ed and his development team. Unlike our previous pitches to entertainment divisions, this discussion wasn't about whether the concept was viable—we had already proven that through successful execution. It was about how our proven model could be adapted for cable television while maintaining the authenticity and interactive elements that made it distinctive.

"We're not interested in turning this into a conventional travel series," Wilson emphasized during our meeting. "What makes *Around the World for Free* compelling is precisely what makes it different—the authentic interactions, the vulnerability, the audience participation. We want to preserve those elements in the storytelling while making the series available to television viewers."

His understanding of what made our project valuable was refreshing after so many executives who had tried to force the concept into familiar formats. Wilson saw the potential in embracing its unconventional qualities rather than attempting to normalize them.

The arrangement he proposed was innovative: WGN America would adapt our existing content into eleven one-hour episodes, creating a television series that would be airing on their network in prime time. They would provide post-production resources to reshape our raw footage into a television format while preserving its authentic quality.

Most importantly, this wasn't just a licensing deal where we would sell rights and walk away. We would serve as executive producers, maintaining creative control over how the content was adapted. The interactive format and platform would remain our property, with WGN controlling the TV rights.

"Think of this as a partnership rather than a traditional network deal," Wilson explained. "We provide the television platform and production resources as needed; you provide the innovative content and storytelling. Together, we create something neither of us could develop independently."

The financial terms were equally groundbreaking. "I'm giving you guys the international rights," Ed told us. "You deserve them." While most networks would easily be able to negotiate these rights away from us, he handed them to us as a gift. On top of that, he immediately called his friends at Reveille (one of the largest international distribution companies), hoping to secure a deal with them.

As we finalized the agreement, I reflected on the irony of the situation. After months of rejection from networks that couldn't categorize our concept, we had created something so distinctive that a forward-thinking executive was now approaching us on our terms. The very qualities that had made *Around the World for Free* difficult to fit into existing frameworks were precisely what made it valuable in a media landscape seeking innovation.

Zsolt took on the management and post-supervision of these episodes for WGN. Adapting our content for television presented new challenges. We had hundreds of hours of footage—some beautifully shot in optimal conditions, some captured in difficult circumstances with limited equipment. We had daily web updates, weekly *The Early Show* segments, and countless moments of authentic human connection documented on our platform (AroundTheWorldForFree.com) throughout the journey.

The challenge wasn't finding compelling content but determining how to distill this vast archive into eleven cohesive episodes that would engage television viewers. We needed to balance narrative clarity with authentic representation of the journey's improvisational nature.

Throughout this process, Wilson remained committed to preserving what made *Around the World for Free* unique. When traditional television instincts might have pushed toward more structured storytelling or glossier production value, he consistently advocated for maintaining the project's distinctive voice and approach.

"The polish isn't what makes this compelling," he observed during a review of early episode cuts. "It's the authenticity of the experience and the genuine human connections. Let's not sacrifice that for conventional television aesthetics."

This perspective aligned perfectly with our vision but represented a departure from typical cable network approaches. Wilson was essentially betting that audiences would connect with content that felt genuine rather than produced, that prioritized authentic human experience over manufactured drama or visual spectacle.

As we approached the series premiere date, WGN developed a marketing strategy that emphasized the backstory that this was a real-time show originally airing digitally.

## 100 Countries and Counting

The day before the premiere, Wilson called with unexpected news that would transform the project's reach and impact.

"I've been talking with the international distribution company Reveille about *Around the World for Free*," he began. "There's significant interest in territories beyond the U.S. market."

This potential had never been part of our original vision or subsequent planning.

But Wilson had recognized an opportunity we hadn't considered. "The human stories you've captured transcend cultural boundaries," he explained.

The conversation had evolved rapidly, with Reveille expressing strong interest in representing the series worldwide.

## A NETWORK DEAL

"I can't promise anything yet," Wilson cautioned, "but I wanted you to know these discussions are happening. If they move forward, it could significantly expand the project's reach and impact."

Just one day later, as the series premiered on WGN America to strong initial ratings, Wilson called again. He had negotiated preliminary terms with Reveille for international distribution rights, subject to our approval as content creators and executive producers.

The structure was a revenue-share with Reveille rather than a simple acquisition fee. Reveille believed the series could potentially reach over 100 countries across multiple continents, introducing our concept of authentic, connection-based travel to audiences worldwide.

This development was almost too remarkable to process. The project that dozens of executives had rejected as too unconventional for American audiences was now being positioned for global distribution. The concept that "wouldn't work" within traditional frameworks was proving valuable precisely because it offered something different from conventional travel programming.

Within weeks of the WGN America premiere, international deals began materializing. First in English-speaking territories like Australia, the UK, and Canada, then expanding to European markets, Latin America, and parts of Asia. Watching our journey resonate with audiences around the world was overwhelmingly gratifying. We got messages from viewers in dozens of countries describing how the series had influenced their perspective on travel and the world, cultural exchange, and human connection. Some were inspired to attempt their own experiments in connection-based travel, others to engage more authentically with different cultures in their own communities.

This international success created financial opportunities beyond anything we had anticipated. The revenue-sharing model meant that each new territory generated additional returns, creating a foundation for Around The World Productions.

The success of the WGN adaptation and international distribution caught the attention of CBS, which had provided our initial platform through *The Early Show*. Now, seeing the project's evolution from experimental concept to proven format with global reach, they approached us about developing additional seasons with full network backing.

This offer represented something extraordinary—a full-circle return to the network that had provided our initial platform, now with recognition and resources commensurate with what we had proven possible. The concept that hadn't fit existing categories had created its own category, compelling traditional media to adapt rather than requiring us to conform. Around this time CBS Interactive was being formed, and doing stuff on the web was "starting" to become a thing.

The structure CBS proposed was comprehensive: they would fund production of new seasons, each with a different host, broadcast weekly segments on *The Early Show*, feature the content across all CBS digital platforms, and potentially develop primetime specials if the projects gained sufficient traction. They would provide technical resources for enhanced interactive features on CBS.com while allowing us to preserve creative control and ownership of the core concept.

More importantly, this validated our fundamental premise: that authentic human connection transcends cultural and economic boundaries, that vulnerability creates opportunities for meaningful exchange, and that audiences respond to genuine experiences more powerfully than to manufactured content.

This offer represented something extraordinary—a full-circle return to the network that had first platformed us, but now with recognition and resources commensurate with what we had proven possible. It wasn't the validation we had sought, but it was meaningful nonetheless. The concept that hadn't fit existing categories had created its own category, compelling traditional media to adapt rather than requiring us to conform.

As we began developing this second iteration with CBS, we maintained the project's core principles while expanding its scope and technical capabilities. The interactive platform evolved to incorporate emerging social media tools, enhancing audience participation opportunities while preserving the authentic human connections that had defined the original journey.

Burton and I determined that for this second season, another traveler should take the lead—Jeff Schroeder, a former *Big Brother* Star with the perfect combination of adaptability, authentic engagement skills, and comfort with vulnerability. I would transition to an executive producer role, applying everything we had learned to create an even more compelling interactive experience.

This evolution from host/traveler to executive producer represented a natural progression in my journey from reality contestant to content creator. Each step—from Amazing Race winner to PineRidge host/producer to *Around the World for Free* creator and participant—had built toward this role, being comfortable wearing whatever hat was needed to make the project a success.

The second season proved even more successful than the first, benefiting from Jeff's Star power, enhanced production resources, expanded interactive capabilities, and the lessons we had learned through our original experiment. CBS's full engagement across platforms along with a massive sponsorship from AT&T generated broader audience awareness, while our refined interactive model created deeper engagement with participants.

This success led to a third season with *Survivor* winner Parvarti Shallow, with CBS increasing investment and expanding distribution channels. *Around the World for Free* had evolved from experimental concept to proven format, from rejected pitch to multi-season, globally distributed content.

Throughout this period of rapid growth and evolution, Burton, Zsolt, and I maintained our focus on the fundamental values that had defined the project from its inception: real, raw, authentic storytelling. Despite increased resources and expanded technical capabilities, we ensured that each iteration preserved these essential qualities rather than succumbing to conventional television production approaches.

This commitment to authenticity became our defining characteristic as Around the World Productions expanded beyond its namesake project to develop additional concepts that applied similar principles to different contexts. We weren't just creating travel content; we were pioneering how audiences watched, interacted with, while sometimes becoming part of the actual story itself

Reflecting on the journey from initial concept to international success, I was struck by how each rejection had ultimately directed us toward more authentic alignment with our vision. If any of those early pitches had been accepted—if we had secured traditional production funding and distribution from the beginning—*Around the World for Free* would likely have become a conventional travel series, losing the very qualities that made it distinctive and valuable.

Instead, necessity had forced innovation. Limited resources had compelled authenticity. Rejection from established systems had required us to create our own framework, one that preserved what mattered most while discarding conventional approaches that didn't serve our purpose.

What had once been simple badges of honor—wearing those rejections as proof we were onto something different—had evolved into something far more valuable: the freedom to create content on our own terms without conforming to industry expectations that would have limited what was possible.

What had begun as a simple question—"Could you do it for free?"—had evolved into something far more significant: a reimagining of how travel content could be created, how audiences could participate in experiences rather than merely consuming them, and how authentic human connection could transcend both economic transaction and cultural boundaries.

The international success of *Around the World for Free* represented more than professional achievement or financial return. It validated a fundamental belief that had guided my journey from the beginning: that the most meaningful experiences emerge not from abundance of resources but from authenticity of engagement; not from careful planning but from vulnerable improvisation; not from conventional wisdom but from the courage to imagine different possibilities.

As Around the World Productions continued developing innovative content and pioneering new approaches to audience engagement, I carried this lesson forward: that rejection often redirects you toward more perfect alignment with your authentic path, that constraints frequently catalyze creativity more effectively than abundance, and that the most valuable opportunities sometimes emerge from the very circumstances that initially appear as obstacles.

The path from Georgetown, Massachusetts to Brazil to Germany to Boston to St. John to *The Amazing Race* to PineRidge to global success had never been direct or predictable. But each apparent detour had contributed something essential to creating content that would ultimately reach

# A NETWORK DEAL

audiences in over 100 countries and help reshape how media engaged with authentic storytelling.

And it had all begun with a natural disaster in El Salvador shutting down our surf documentary and an offhand comment at a screening event in Jacksonville, and a simple question that no one had adequately answered: Could you do it for free?

The answer, it turned out, was yes—not just traveling around the world without money, but creating a new model for content that prioritized human connection over production value, authentic engagement over manufactured drama, and participation over passive consumption.

That "yes" had opened doors no one could have predicted, creating opportunities not just for Around the World Productions but for a reimagining of how media could function in an increasingly connected global community. The badge of honor earned through countless rejections had become something far more valuable: the freedom to create without conforming to expectations that would have limited what was possible.

And that freedom, ultimately, was worth more than any conventional success could have provided.

> "Sometimes the most significant inspirations emerge from genuine human connections."

# 17

# CAREER SHIFTS

Success changes things, but not always in the ways you might expect. As Around the World Productions flourished, producing multiple seasons of our flagship series *Around the World For Free* and developing new concepts that applied similar interactive elements to different networks and shows, my professional life expanded in directions I couldn't have anticipated when we first embarked on that experimental journey without money.

### *DreamJobbing*: The Next Evolution

Burton and I had built something significant—not just successful production company, but a genuinely innovative approach to creating and distributing content. We had proven that authentic engagement could generate more meaningful audience connection than polished production, that real stories could be more compelling than manufactured drama, and that participation created deeper investment than passive consumption.

These principles guided our work as we developed new projects, expanded our team, and navigated an industry in the midst of profound transformation. Traditional television was evolving rapidly in response to digital platforms, changing audience behaviors, and emerging technologies. Our experience straddling conventional and interactive media positioned us uniquely to bridge these evolving worlds.

Around 2010, this evolving landscape presented a new opportunity—one that would take me in yet another unexpected direction. A concept called *DreamJobbing* began taking shape. The premise was simple but powerful: creating opportunities for people to experience their dream jobs through short-term immersion experiences.

*DreamJobbing* combined elements that had proven successful in our previous work—authentic human experiences, genuine connection, meaningful transformation—while exploring professional aspirations rather than travel or cultural exchange. It allowed participants to step briefly into roles they dreamed of occupying—things like a Social Buzz Reporter for VH1, a Producer for a CBS Network Show, a Tour Reporter for *Nitro Circus*, a Guest Chef on *The Rachael Ray Show*, and a backup singer for Michael Bolton. We created content around these experiences while potentially opening doors to new career paths.

This concept resonated with me personally. My own career had been anything but linear—from market analyst to bartender to Amazing Race contestant to stock footage salesman to host-producer to co-founder of an innovative production company. Each unexpected turn had contributed something essential to my development, often in ways I couldn't have anticipated at the time.

*DreamJobbing* formalized this philosophy of career exploration, creating structured opportunities for people to step outside conventional paths and discover possibilities they might never have considered otherwise. It wasn't just content; it was a potential catalyst for life transformation—exactly the kind of meaningful impact I had always hoped my work might achieve.

Developing this platform required new partnerships and skills. We joined forces with Lisa Hennessy, another reality TV veteran with extensive production experience helping build Mark Burnett Productions, bringing her complementary expertise and fresh perspective. Together, we built *DreamJobbing* from concept to functioning platform, creating opportunities across industries and documenting the transformative experiences that resulted.

Each *DreamJobbing* opportunity worked like this. We would launch the opportunity via as much press as possible. Anyone could go to the *DreamJobbing* platform and apply with a 60-second video. People would share their videos through their social networks, gaining likes, etc. One person was chosen and then we would follow that person as they embarked on this once-in-a-lifetime experience. It was pretty awesome!

The early response was encouraging. Partnerships with major brands and entertainment properties provided resources to create meaningful experiences. Participants shared powerful stories of insight and transformation. Media outlets highlighted the innovative approach to career exploration and content creation.

But beneath this promising surface, challenges were emerging. The business model—combining content production, platform development, and experience creation—together with the technical infrastructure ended up costing more money than we took in from the brands.

Despite creating meaningful experiences and compelling content, the financial foundation remained precarious. We relied on the brands paying us for putting their DreamJob together and creating the earned media from all the press, social media, and professional content produced. And although everyone from the brands to the participants to the audience loved it...we could never make enough money to turn a profit.

By 2015, these tensions were becoming increasingly evident. The platform had achieved meaningful impact for individual participants and created valuable content, but the underlying business model wasn't achieving the sustainability we had envisioned. Something needed to change—either the fundamental approach or our involvement with it.

This period coincided with personal transitions as well. I was close to getting married, beginning a new chapter that inevitably shifted my perspective on work-life balance and long-term priorities. The constant hustle of entrepreneurial ventures and production schedules, while exhilarating, demanded sacrifices that seemed increasingly significant in this new context.

As *DreamJobbing* continued facing sustainability challenges, an unexpected opportunity emerged. Shane Farley, who had produced me on the Rosie O'Donnell Show after my Amazing Race win and had risen to become an executive producer on the Rachael Ray Show and greenlit Rach to the Rescue (a spin-off of *Around the World For Free*), reached out about a potential role on his new show he would be executive producing... *The Steve Harvey Show*.

The position wasn't one I would have envisioned for myself—running the field team for a daily talk show rather than creating travel content or interactive real-time media I was known for. But it offered stability during an uncertain period and the chance to apply my production skills in a different context with a trusted colleague.

"I know you've never worked on talk shows," Shane acknowledged when describing the opportunity. "But you know how to run field production better than most people in this industry. That's exactly what we need for the field segments—finding and telling real stories that resonate with Steve and our audience."

His assessment was insightful. While the format and structure of daily talk television differed dramatically from the content I had been creating, the underlying principles remained consistent: identifying authentic human stories, creating conditions for genuine connection, and capturing moments that resonated emotionally rather than merely entertaining.

I accepted the position, stepping away from the day-to-day operations at *DreamJobbing* while promising Lisa and Burton to do my best to work nights and weekends to help keep the brand alive. Even though it was hard to walk away from a project I invested so much hard work into…I knew it was the right decision. This transition wasn't an abandonment of entrepreneurial ventures but a strategic pivot—an opportunity to apply my skills in a new context while regaining solid financial footing after the uncertainty of recent years.

*The Steve Harvey Show* proved both challenging and rewarding. The pace of daily television production contrasted sharply with the extended timelines of our previous projects. The structured environment of an established show differed from the improvisational approach we had pioneered. The focus on entertainment within familiar formats required adjustment from someone accustomed to creating new frameworks.

Yet the core work—telling compelling human stories—was an area I thrived in. The field team I led became known for segments that were fun, relatable, and emotional. Word had been passed to us that Steve was so busy that many times he was learning about these stories while watching them on screen for the first time with the live audience. So our storytelling became vital to the show. Steve would watch alongside the audience and then do his things interviewing the guests.

This work earned recognition beyond what I had anticipated, culminating in an Emmy nomination that acknowledged the quality of the show produced. The recognition was gratifying, but more meaningful was the confirmation that the principles that had guided my work throughout various formats, shows, and networks—authenticity, human-centric

## CAREER SHIFTS

storytelling, meaningful engagement—translated effectively even within conventional television structures.

After *The Steve Harvey Show*'s successful run, Lisa Hennessy reached out with another opportunity. She and Mark Burnett were bringing back Eco-Challenge. The revamped series would now be for Amazon Prime with Bear Grylls as the host, an ambitious production that combined extreme physical challenges with compelling human stories in remote locations around the world.

After most of the hiring was complete, there were three producing roles they were looking to fill. Producers who they could throw anywhere at any given time and trust they would come back with the story. We were like one-man bands running around a jungle wherever something exciting might be happening. The project needed someone with both production expertise and experience navigating challenging environments—a description that matched my background precisely.

This role represented yet another evolution, not hosting or creating my own content, but helping shape a major production led by others. It drew on everything from my *Amazing Race* experience to my work producing travel content to my field production skills developed on *The Steve Harvey Show*. Once again, what might have appeared as career diversions had actually been perfect preparation for an unexpected opportunity.

The production proved as challenging as anticipated, filming through over 100 villages across Fiji, in extreme conditions, and with complex logistical requirements. But it also provided the opportunity to return to the kind of immersive, location-based content that had always engaged me most deeply—capturing real stories in remote areas of the globe.

Just as this project was nearing completion in early 2020, the world changed dramatically. COVID-19 emerged as a global pandemic, transforming every aspect of daily life and bringing the entertainment industry to an unprecedented standstill. Productions shut down, teams dispersed to work remotely, and the future of media creation became suddenly uncertain.

Like countless others, I found myself navigating this new reality with more questions than answers. The pandemic's impact on production schedules and methods was immediate and profound. Projects in development were paused indefinitely. Established shows struggled to adapt to remote production requirements. The path forward for content producers became unclear in ways no one could have anticipated.

During this period of professional uncertainty and global transformation, a seemingly small family event occurred that would redirect my path yet again—this time toward what would become my most meaningful work yet.

## A Niece's Problem Becomes a Calling

A few months prior to COVID unleashing on the globe, my niece, Isabelle, visited from Chippewa Falls, Wisconsin. She was a high school student approaching the critical college selection process that would shape her educational future. Her family (like many of the families across the country) had limited resources for college exploration. It's expensive for a family to travel to another state or far away to visit a campus. They could afford exactly one trip to visit potential schools, making the stakes of that single journey extraordinarily high.

Isabelle (and her mom, my older sister Andrea) came to stay with me in Los Angeles, and we spent a week visiting various college campuses in Southern California. The experience was both enlightening and concerning. While the visits provided valuable insights into the schools we explored, they also highlighted a fundamental inequity in the college selection process: students with financial resources could visit numerous campuses, gaining firsthand experience of each environment, while those with limited means often made life-changing decisions based on websites, brochures, and (if lucky) perhaps a single campus visit.

As we drove between campuses, Isabelle expressed frustration with this reality. "I want to visit schools in New England too, where you and Mom grew up," she said. "And there are programs in other states that sound perfect for what I want to study. But we just can't afford to travel to all these places."

Her mother—my sister Andrea—confirmed this limitation. "This trip to California is it," she explained. "If it wasn't for you being here, we probably wouldn't have been able to do even this much campus exploration. She has to make her college decision based on the resources we have."

This conversation struck me deeply. The inequity wasn't just financial; it was informational. Students like Isabelle were making one of life's most consequential decisions with dramatically less firsthand knowledge than their more affluent peers. This disadvantage would shape not just their educational experience but potentially their entire professional trajectory.

As a media creator who had spent years developing innovative approaches to sharing authentic stories, I immediately recognized a potential solution. "What if," I suggested to Isabelle, "instead of you traveling to all these campuses, we could bring the campuses to you? What if there was a way to experience the location, real culture, and community of schools across the country without having to physically visit each one?"

The idea began taking shape organically. Each week, Isabelle and I would connect virtually, exploring different colleges together through their websites. I would guide her through online resources, helping her evaluate potential matches for her interests and goals. But the limitations of existing resources quickly became apparent—websites and virtual tours provided superficial information, but rarely captured the authentic culture and community that made each institution unique.

This gap between available resources and actual need presented a clear opportunity. If traditional college search tools weren't providing what students like Isabelle required, perhaps there was a way to create something that would—content that captured the genuine experience of each campus through the perspectives of actual students rather than glossy marketing materials.

The concept for what would become *The College Tour* emerged from this personal challenge. It would be a series that explored colleges and universities across America, told through the authentic voices of current students who could speak to the real experience of attending each institution. Not promotional content created by marketing departments, but genuine insights from those actually living the college experience in all its complexity.

This concept aligned perfectly with principles that had guided my work for years: authentic human stories rather than manufactured presentations; diverse perspectives rather than singular narratives; meaningful information that could genuinely impact viewers' lives rather than merely entertaining them.

As I developed this idea further, researching the college search landscape and consulting with education professionals, I discovered that the need was even greater than I had initially recognized. Millions of students faced the same challenges as Isabelle—not just those with financial limitations, but international students considering American universities, first-generation college applicants without family guidance, and countless others for whom extensive campus visits were impractical or impossible.

The pandemic only intensified this need. With physical campus visits suddenly restricted or eliminated entirely, even students with financial resources found themselves making college decisions without the firsthand experiences previous generations had relied upon. Institutions scrambled to create virtual alternatives, but few had the resources or expertise to develop truly engaging content that captured their unique qualities.

*The College Tour* represented a potential solution to this critical problem—one that leveraged everything I had learned throughout my unconventional career path. The authentic storytelling approaches developed through PineRidge. The production efficiencies mastered on *Around the World for Free*. The field production techniques, which were refined on *The Steve Harvey Show*. The logistical capabilities honed during *The World's Toughest Race*. All these seemingly disparate experiences had prepared me to create content that could genuinely transform the college search process for students everywhere.

As I began developing the concept in detail—outlining format, researching potential production approaches, exploring distribution options—I recognized that this project represented something different from previous ventures. It wasn't just compelling content or innovative production; it was a genuine educational resource with the potential to impact one of life's most consequential decisions for millions of students.

The timing, while challenging due to the pandemic, also presented unique opportunities. Institutions were actively seeking new ways to reach prospective students when traditional recruitment methods had been disrupted. Students and families needed alternative approaches to college exploration when physical visits were restricted. The industry had been forced to embrace remote production methods that could be adapted for this new concept.

What had begun as a personal response to my niece's challenge was evolving into a fully realized production concept with significant potential impact. As I developed the format further—episodes focused on individual institutions, segments featuring diverse student perspectives, content available across multiple platforms—I became increasingly convinced that *The College Tour* represented not just another production opportunity but potentially my most meaningful professional contribution yet.

As I prepared to transform this concept from idea to reality—navigating the production challenges of a pandemic, building partnerships with colleges, developing distribution strategies for reaching students who needed this resource most—I felt a clarity of purpose that transcended previous ventures. This wasn't just about creating entertaining content or building a successful business; it was about addressing a fundamental inequity in one of society's most important systems.

The journey from selling calendars door-to-door to developing a series that might transform educational access had been neither direct nor predictable. But standing at this new threshold, I could see how each step—even those that had seemed like setbacks or diversions at the time—had been essential preparation for what now felt like the most meaningful work of my career.

And it had all begun with a simple family moment: a niece visiting her uncle, sharing her frustration about college search limitations, and a TV producer recognizing that the skills he had developed throughout an unconventional career might offer a solution that could benefit not just one student but potentially millions.

Sometimes the most significant inspirations emerge not from industry trends or market analysis but from trying to solve another human's problem—in this case, the desire to help a family member navigate a challenge that reflected a broader societal issue. As I moved forward with developing *The College Tour*, this personal foundation remained central, reminding me that the most meaningful work often emerges from the intersection of professional capability and personal purpose.

The journey was about to take another unexpected turn—one that would lead to campus quads rather than foreign countries, to conversations with students rather than negotiations with network executives, to content that educated rather than merely entertained. And somehow, despite its apparent departure from previous ventures, it felt like the most natural next chapter in a story that had always been about authentic connection, meaningful engagement, and the power of real stories.

*The College Tour* was about to begin.

> "The power of relationships will cultivate throughout your entire career."

# 18

# BUILDING *THE COLLEGE TOUR*

With the concept for *The College Tour* clearly defined and Isabelle's challenge fresh in my mind, I faced the practical reality of actually making this happen during a global pandemic. Nothing about traditional television production worked anymore. But maybe that was exactly what we needed.

The timing couldn't have been more challenging—or more perfect. Around the World Productions had built an incredible run, working with Travel Channel, CBS, and other major networks and platforms. But then life intervened. Burton, a true Texan, had moved to Texas because he wanted to make sure his daughters had a Texas passport and be closer to his family. So Burton moved to Texas, and while nothing was officially different, the reality was that two business partners who had been grinding it out together in LA had now been seperated for awhile.

When COVID hit, it had been close to two years since Burton and I had worked on a project together. I was sitting in my garage, talking to Burton, both of us feeling like something essential was missing.

## Making It Work in Impossible Times

I started sharing with him about Isabelle's visit a few months earlier and her frustration about trying to figure out where to go to college. Sitting in that garage, I said to Burton, "There might be a show here." I explained the whole challenge of college search, and Burton immediately loved it. More than that, he was like, "Man, we haven't worked together in a couple years. This doesn't feel right." I asked, "Shall we do this, bro?"...and off we went.

After building out the initial deck and trailer, we called Lisa to see if she was interested in joining this mission while bringing back the original

*DreamJobbing* team. Lisa got the idea immediately and suggested it could be a good fit for Adrenaline Films. She and Mike Murray had a thirty+ year history in the business—Mike had been one of the original directors of photography on *Survivor* Season 1 and had built Adrenaline Films in Orlando into a beautiful studio serving Universal, Disney, and countless other clients.

But we faced a fundamental problem: we had to completely rethink how to produce a show when you couldn't travel normally, when campuses were sometimes closed or restricted, when everyone was figuring out safety protocols on the fly. The constraints forced us to strip everything down to what really mattered: getting authentic student stories without all the usual production bloat.

Small crews. Remote preparation with students before we arrived. Quick, efficient shoots that respected campus health guidelines. It wasn't glamorous, but it worked. Sometimes the best solutions come from having no other choice.

One critical addition came early when I found Beth Cohen. When I explained what we wanted to do with *The College Tour*, she got it in two seconds. "Let me be your head of partnerships," she said. Beth had the perfect combination of educational background and media experience, and she was instrumental in getting the colleges on board and driving this out-of-the-box idea into the higher education marketplace.

The team also included Joan McCord, who had run PineRidge Film and Television under Jerry Smith. Joan always joked she was half in retirement, but I convinced her to come on as a supervising producer, handling much of our pre-production work. And there was Martine Olarte, Mike's right-hand at Adrenaline Films.

What struck me was how the media business disruption brought out the best in people who'd been around the block. Everyone was willing to roll up their sleeves, saying, "Let's not worry so much about profit and money right now. Can we make this show the way we want to make it?"

## The First Season: Learning on the Fly

Finding universities willing to partner with an unproven concept during a crisis required a completely different approach than anything I'd done before. These weren't entertainment companies looking for content deals—they were educational institutions with entirely different priorities and decision-making processes. We had to learn their language, understand their concerns, and prove that what we were creating would genuinely serve their prospective students.

Our first episode was Fort Lewis College in Durango, Colorado—let's call it a pilot, but it was a real episode. That first shoot felt different than everything else because we were going through everything for the first time. It was COVID, so we couldn't film any students inside without masks, which wouldn't work for television. Fires were burning everywhere in northern Colorado, blowing smoke down to the area of the college, filling the air with smoke, limiting where we could film outside. Then a hailstorm ripped through campus. Mother Earth threw everything at us during that first shoot.

I'd originally thought I didn't want the students to sound rehearsed, so we'd get their basic story and then just talk it through on camera. But I realized on the fly that we needed scripts—their story but actual scripts where they knew exactly what they were going to say. I was calling students mid-production: "I know we were going to shoot you today, but let's film tomorrow. Let's work on the script tonight."

We filmed Florida Tech next and then episode #3 was big. Arizona State University took a chance on us next, and they got it immediately—here was a way to reach students who couldn't visit campus, to share their story through the voices of actual students rather than marketing departments. If we could capture the essence of one of the country's largest universities through student perspectives, we could make this work anywhere.

The students blew me away. Their stories were genuine, compelling, and informative in ways no brochure could match. Each person brought a different perspective—different backgrounds, different reasons for choosing ASU, different experiences on campus. Together, they painted a picture of the university that felt real rather than manufactured.

The first season showed us something crucial: it didn't matter what type of school you were—big or small, this would work. After ASU came Delaware Valley University, another small school. Then the University of Illinois, Champaign. Then, there was a school called Salus. Then, the University of Connecticut. The diversity proved our concept.

As more schools got interested, I knew we had to establish some non-negotiables. The students' voices had to stay central—no letting institutional messaging take over. We needed diverse perspectives in every episode, not just the obvious success stories. Production quality had to be consistently high, whether we were filming at the University of Texas or a small community college. And most importantly, this content had to be accessible to students everywhere, not locked behind paywalls or restricted platforms.

That last point mattered more than any business consideration. What good would it do to create this resource if the students who needed it most couldn't access it? Amazon Prime Video became our first major distribution partner, giving us a legitimate platform while keeping the content freely available to anyone with an internet connection. And we built out a robust website, TheCollegeTour.com, where the episodes lived, where students can take fun classes to help them in their search, and much more.

## The Messages That Mattered

The feedback started coming almost immediately, and it confirmed everything we'd hoped the show could accomplish. A student from rural Mississippi wrote: "My family can't afford to visit colleges outside our state, but through your show, I discovered a program in Colorado that's perfect for what I want to study. I've applied for and received a scholarship I never would have known about otherwise."

But the most satisfying success story was Isabelle herself. While watching our Arizona State episode, she noticed we featured a student who'd gotten a full ride through Starbucks' scholarship program. Isabelle worked at Starbucks, too, but had no idea this opportunity existed. She looked into it, applied, and got a full scholarship to ASU. Watching that episode literally changed the trajectory of her education. That's when I knew we were onto something real.

Another message that stuck with me came from Alabama: "I always thought college was for other people—people with more money, better grades, different backgrounds. But watching real students who look like me, who came from places like my hometown, who faced similar challenges... it made me believe I could belong there too. I've now applied to three schools I first discovered through your show."

What became clear to me as we built *The College Tour* was how it represented the power of relationships cultivated throughout my entire career. Lisa and I had worked together on *DreamJobbing*. Burton and I went back to Around the World Productions. Zsolt Luka, who runs distribution for *The College Tour*, went back to PineRidge days with me. Same with Joan McCord. The relationship thread ran everywhere.

Being likable and maintaining relationships had become one of my core principles. Anyone I'd ever worked with, I could call up tomorrow, and we would pick up where we left off. This is one of the most important lessons I share with college students today. Keep your relationships strong. This was one of the most important lessons I could pass on.

As we expanded beyond that first handful of episodes, the diversity of schools participating became one of our biggest strengths. Major research universities, tiny liberal arts colleges, urban campuses, rural settings, HBCUs, and technical schools—each brought something different to the series while fitting into the same format that let viewers compare their options meaningfully.

## The Hundred Episode Mark

By 2022, we'd reached a milestone that felt surreal: our 100th episode. Standing on that hundredth campus, I thought about how far we'd come from those early Zoom calls with Isabelle, frustrated about her limited college search options.

Universities that had initially seen us as a pandemic workaround were now recognizing that authentic student perspectives offered insights even campus visits couldn't provide. Students confirmed this in their feedback—the show gave them a deeper understanding of campus culture and student experience than they could get from a day-long visit or a glossy brochure.

What had started as a solution to my niece's immediate problem had become something much bigger: a permanent part of how students explore their college options. The series was streaming millions of views, universities were reporting real recruitment benefits, and most importantly, students were making better-informed decisions about their educational futures.

## The Full Circle

Standing on that hundredth campus, I realized we'd built exactly what I'd always wanted to create: something that entertained while it educated, that engaged while it informed, that could genuinely transform trajectories rather than just occupy attention.

*The College Tour* represented everything I'd learned along the way: authentic storytelling from my PineRidge days, resourceful production from *Around the World for Free*, field production skills from Steve Harvey, and the understanding that constraints often force the best innovations. All those seemingly random career turns had somehow prepared me perfectly for this moment.

What started as helping one student navigate her college search had become a bridge connecting millions of students to educational opportunities they might never have discovered otherwise. We were expanding possibilities across geographic boundaries, economic limitations, and a simple lack of awareness.

And that felt like the most meaningful thing I could imagine building.

> "When you strategically leverage networking, you can create extraordinary opportunities."

# 19

# THE COLLEGE-TO-CAREER PLAYBOOK

As *The College Tour* grew beyond its initial concept, my presence on campuses evolved as well. While my primary role remained executive producing and hosting the series, universities increasingly invited me to speak directly with their students. What began as occasional conversations with film and television departments expanded to campus-wide presentations, where I shared insights from my unconventional career path with students preparing for their professional journeys.

## The Golden Ticket: Leveraging Student Status

These speaking engagements revealed something unexpected. While students were genuinely interested in my media experiences, they were even more eager for practical guidance on navigating the transition from college to career. The questions following my presentations rarely focused on reality TV or my hosting and producing experience; they centered on how to find meaningful work, build professional connections, and create opportunities in competitive industries.

This consistent pattern prompted me to develop what eventually became known as *The College-to-Career Playbook* (available at www.AlexBoylan.com)—a practical framework for leveraging the unique advantages of student status to build professional relationships before graduation. The approach wasn't theoretical; it was based on my own experiences and observations of what worked in real-world professional contexts.

The foundational premise was simple but powerful: Being a college student represents a unique advantage in professional networking that disappears immediately upon graduation. When students understand and strategically leverage this temporary asset, they can build relationships that create extraordinary opportunities before they enter the competitive job market.

"You are currently holding a golden ticket," I will tell students during these presentations. "Your status as a student gives you access to professionals who will be much harder to reach after graduation. People who might ignore an email from a job seeker will often respond to a student seeking information or advice. This advantage has a strict expiration date—the moment you receive your diploma."

This concept surprised many students. They typically view their student status as a disadvantage—a marker of inexperience or incomplete credentials—rather than a strategic asset with temporary but significant value. Shifting this perspective was the first crucial step in helping them recognize and utilize their current position.

The playbook I shared evolved through dozens of campus presentations, refined by student feedback and examples of successful implementation. The process consisted of several key components, each building on the previous steps to create a comprehensive approach to relationship-building before graduation.

First, students needed to establish a professional presence, primarily through LinkedIn, that authentically embraced their student identity rather than attempting to appear more experienced than they were. "Don't try to look like a seasoned professional on your profile," I advised. "Be proudly and authentically a student. Wear your college gear in your profile photo. Show your campus in the background. Your student identity is your advantage—highlight it rather than hide it."

This authentic student presence served as the foundation for strategic outreach to professionals in their fields of interest. I provided a methodical approach: identify target companies and individuals, research their backgrounds and recent work, and prepare thoughtful, specific questions that demonstrated genuine interest rather than generic networking attempts.

The outreach itself followed a consistent format I had seen work repeatedly. A brief email or LinkedIn message that:

1. Clearly identified the sender as a student at a specific institution
2. Expressed genuine interest in the recipient's work or expertise

3. Requested a short (10-minute) conversation to ask specific questions
4. Emphasized that this is for a class assignment which is the truth because I am assigning it to you :), not a job request

"The key is brevity and clarity," I explained. "Professionals receive dozens or hundreds of messages daily. Your communication needs to be concise, specific, and immediately identifiable as coming from a student seeking information rather than someone wanting something more substantial."

What surprised many students was the high response rate this approach typically generated. Professionals who might ignore conventional networking attempts or job inquiries often responded positively to students clearly seeking information for educational purposes. The time constraint—requesting just 10 minutes—made the ask reasonable, while the student identification created an opportunity for the professional to be helpful without substantial commitment.

Once these initial conversations were secured—whether via phone, video call, or occasionally in person—the playbook provides guidance for making them meaningful. Preparation is essential: researching the professional's background, understanding their organization, preparing thoughtful questions, and being ready to share relevant interests without dominating the conversation.

"The single most important question to ask," I emphasized, "is some version of: 'If you were in my position, graduating next year with my interests and background, what would you focus on doing now?' This question transforms the conversation from information-gathering to targeted advice from someone who understands the field you're trying to enter."

The follow-up process was critical. Within 24 hours of any conversation, students should send a personalized thank-you note (ideally a physical card for memorable impact sent via FedEx to make sure they receive it) referencing specific insights gained from the discussion. This immediate acknowledgment demonstrated professionalism while reinforcing the connection established during the conversation.

But the most powerful element of the playbook—and what differentiated it from conventional networking advice—was the long-term relationship cultivation strategy. Rather than treating these initial conversations as one-time interactions, students were encouraged to establish systems for maintaining meaningful contact over months or years before graduation.

## From Contact to Connection

"The goal isn't to become pen pals," I clarified. "It's to establish yourself as someone genuinely interested in their field and their work, someone who stays engaged. These periodic, meaningful touchpoints keep you in their awareness without becoming intrusive."

When implemented consistently across multiple professionals in a student's field of interest, this approach created actual connections—not merely a collection of contacts, but relationships with people who had provided guidance, received thoughtful follow-up, and maintained awareness of the student over time.

The culmination comes approximately three months before graduation, when students can reach out to these established connections: "I wanted to let you know I'll be graduating this spring and am exploring opportunities in [specific area]. Our conversations have been incredibly helpful in shaping my direction, and I'd welcome any suggestions you might have as I begin this transition."

This message, coming from someone the professional had already advised and who had maintained thoughtful contact, often generated extraordinary responses—job leads, introductions to hiring managers, and sometimes direct offers. The relationship foundation transformed what might otherwise have been a cold job inquiry into a warm connection with someone already invested in the student's success.

One particularly memorable example came from a student at a small liberal arts college who had implemented the playbook throughout his junior year, building relationships with professionals at three companies where he hoped to work. Three months before graduation, he reached out to these connections as suggested. Within weeks, he had interview opportunities at all three organizations, ultimately receiving two job offers at significantly higher starting salaries than typical for graduates from his program.

"The crazy thing," he wrote, "is that neither of these positions was publicly advertised. They were created after my connections advocated for bringing me in. Without those relationships, I wouldn't even have known these opportunities existed."

This outcome exemplified the playbook's central premise: the most valuable opportunities often exist outside formal application processes, accessible primarily through relationships established before they're needed.

What resonated most with both students and educators was the playbook's emphasis on agency rather than credentials. While students couldn't control the prestige of their institution or their family connections, they could control their approach to building professional relationships before graduation. This shift from passive recipient of career services to active architect of professional connections empowered students across diverse circumstances.

During one campus presentation, a student asked whether this approach still worked in an increasingly automated hiring landscape. My response emphasized the enduring value of human connection: "Technology has changed how formal applications are processed, but it hasn't changed how humans make decisions about who they want to work with. The most valuable opportunities have always resided in the realm of human relationships rather than formal processes."

This perspective resonated particularly with students from backgrounds traditionally underrepresented in professional networks. One first-generation student expressed this impact powerfully: "Before learning these approaches, I thought professional success depended primarily on where you went to school or who your family knew. I didn't have either advantage. This playbook showed me that I could create my own professional relationships through initiative and authentic engagement."

The playbook, like *The College Tour* itself, represented both culmination and continuation, drawing on everything I had experienced while creating new opportunities I couldn't yet fully envision. What had begun as practical advice shared during campus presentations was evolving into a comprehensive framework with the potential to transform how students approached the crucial transition from education to professional life.

And that transformation was exactly what higher education itself aspired to achieve—not merely conveying knowledge or conferring credentials, but empowering students to create meaningful paths forward regardless of where they began their journeys.

"Genuine resilience is not the capacity to endure challenges, but to find opportunity within them."

# 20

# FATHERHOOD AND LESSONS LEARNED

Life has a way of bringing you full circle, though rarely in ways you might predict. My journey from selling calendars door-to-door on the North Shore of Boston to creating educational content viewed by millions has been anything but linear. Yet at each stage, certain fundamental values have remained constant—values I first learned in that modest home where my father's pastor's salary meant hand-me-down clothes and working for everything I wanted.

## Fatherhood: The Ultimate Perspective Shift

Those early lessons in resourcefulness, determination, and the value of authentic human connection have guided me through every chapter, from Brazilian favelas to German boardrooms, from Caribbean beach bars to television production sets. And now they shape my most important role yet: husband and father.

Marriage changed me in ways I didn't anticipate. After years of globe-trotting adventure and career-focused intensity, building a partnership with someone who shares your journey brings different kinds of growth and fulfillment. The skills that served me well navigating unfamiliar countries—adaptability, communication across differences, genuine curiosity about another's perspective—proved equally valuable in creating a meaningful relationship.

When our son was born in 2024, amid the continuing expansion of *The College Tour*, I experienced a shift in perspective more profound than any previous life transition. Holding this tiny human who depended entirely on our care, I felt a responsibility and connection unlike anything I'd known before.

Fatherhood brought immediate practical changes. Everything demanded more selective consideration of their value relative to their impact on our family life.

But beyond these logistical adjustments, fatherhood prompted deeper reflection on what matters most—both personally and professionally. What values did I want to pass on? What example did I hope to set? What kind of world did I want to help create for his generation?

These questions brought me back to my own upbringing and the foundation my parents had provided, despite our modest circumstances. My father, serving his congregation and community with unwavering commitment, demonstrated daily that meaningful work transcends financial compensation. My mother, managing a household of four children on limited resources, exemplified creativity, resilience, and the ability to create richness beyond material wealth.

Their example had shaped me more profoundly than I'd fully appreciated during my younger years. The work ethic that drove me to sell those calendars door-to-door. The curiosity that led me to embrace unfamiliar cultures in Brazil and Germany. The willingness to start at the bottom—sweeping floors at PineRidge if necessary—to build something meaningful. All of this can be traced back to the values they had instilled through both teaching and living example.

Now, watching my son begin his own journey of discovery, I find myself reflecting on what legacy I hoped to leave—not just professionally through *The College Tour* and other ventures, but personally through the values and perspectives I modeled daily.

Three principles emerged that seemed most essential to pass forward:

First, genuine resilience—not just the capacity to endure challenges, but the ability to find opportunity within them. Throughout my winding path, apparent setbacks had consistently led to unexpected growth. The corporate job that made me miserable led to the St. John adventure that restored my sense of purpose. The *Survivor* rejection coincided with losing my college soccer eligibility, pushing me toward the journey that ultimately connected me with 'Winning' *The Amazing Race*. The countless "no" responses to *Around the World for Free* forced the innovation that made it genuinely groundbreaking.

I want my son to understand that resilience isn't just bouncing back from difficulty; it's recognizing that challenges often redirect you toward paths better aligned with your authentic strengths and values. That lesson—learning to wear "no" as a badge of honor—had transformed apparent obstacles into catalysts for my most meaningful opportunities.

Second, the value of human connection across differences. From living with a host family in Brazil to traveling without money through dozens of countries to capturing student stories across hundreds of diverse institutions, I have consistently found that meaningful connection transcends apparent barriers of language, culture, economics, and background.

I hope my son will grow up recognizing that our differences—whether cultural, socioeconomic, political, or philosophical—needn't divide us when approached with genuine curiosity and respect. The most valuable insights often come from those whose experiences differ most dramatically from our own. That authentic connection across differences creates possibilities that remain inaccessible within homogeneous environments.

Third, the understanding that meaningful work involves contribution beyond personal gain. Throughout my career, the projects that had engaged me most deeply were those that combined professional success with positive impact for others, whether sharing a story about helping a family navigate a challenging situation on *The Steve Harvey Show*, creating transformative adventures through *Around the World for Free*, or expanding educational access through *The College Tour*.

I want my son to recognize that work can be more than an economic transaction—that it could be a vehicle for creating value aligned with your deepest values. That professional success and meaningful contribution aren't opposing forces but complementary aspects of a fulfilling career. The most sustainable satisfaction comes not from what you acquire but from what you create and contribute.

## Recognizing the Journey's Gifts

As I juggle the demands of growing production schedules, speaking engagements, and family responsibilities, I find myself increasingly grateful for the unconventional path that had led to this moment. The diverse skills developed across various roles—from hosting to producing to business development to sales—allowed adaptation to evolving opportunities.

The relationships built throughout my winding journey provided both professional possibilities and personal support.

This gratitude extends particularly to the mentors who had guided critical transitions. I would like to thank Mike Savelyev, who had offered the German internship opportunity that transformed my understanding of international business. Jerry Smith, who had seen potential in the stock footage salesman willing to "sweep floors," provided the foundation for genuine production expertise. Anne O'Grady, who opened the doors to CBS for *Around the World for Free*. The countless others who had offered guidance, opened doors, or simply believed in possibilities I was still learning to envision.

Their collective impact reminded me daily of the responsibility to offer similar guidance to those navigating their own paths—whether students implementing the playbook strategies, young professionals seeking direction in creative fields, or colleagues building new ventures. Mentorship isn't an additional responsibility but an essential aspect of meaningful work, creating value that extends far beyond individual projects or productions.

This perspective informs my continued evolution of *The College Tour* as both an educational platform and a vehicle for student empowerment. Beyond simply showcasing institutions, we increasingly emphasized the diverse pathways students created within these environments—how they transformed educational opportunities into meaningful directions aligned with their unique strengths and values.

My hands-on involvement in *The College Tour* continues despite the project's expanding scale—a commitment that sometimes puzzled industry colleagues accustomed to executive producers delegating responsibilities as series grow. But this direct engagement with the institutions, campuses, and students remained essential to both the project's integrity and my personal fulfillment. If you don't get your hands dirty doing the actual work, you probably don't have a pulse on the business or the market.

Walking across diverse campuses, engaging with students sharing their educational experiences, and helping capture the unique qualities of each institution connected directly to what I found most meaningful in my work: creating content that entertained while educating, that engaged while informing, that potentially transformed trajectories rather than merely occupying attention.

This integration of professional fulfillment and meaningful impact represented what I'd searched for throughout my winding career path—work that didn't feel like "work" in the conventional sense because it aligned so completely with my authentic strengths and values.

"I don't work," I tell students during campus presentations. "I create things I deeply believe in alongside people I like to work with. The effort involved is considerable, but it doesn't feel like work because it's aligned with what matters most to me. That alignment doesn't happen accidentally—it comes from making choices based on values rather than solely on conventional metrics of success." And I chase what excites me. Honestly... this is it more than anything else. If I get excited about it...If I wake up at 4 am thinking about it...I know I am on to something.

This perspective resonated particularly with students questioning traditional careers that prioritize prestige and compensation above personal meaning and societal contribution. Many expressed concern about choosing between financial stability and authentic fulfillment—a dichotomy I navigated throughout my own journey.

"The most sustainable success," I tell them, "comes from finding the intersection between what you're genuinely good at, what you deeply enjoy, and what creates meaningful value for others. That intersection might not be immediately obvious—it certainly wasn't in my case—but exploring diverse experiences with this framework in mind eventually reveals patterns that guide you toward alignment."

This guidance reflects what I wished someone had told my younger self during periods of uncertainty—when I was grinding through market analyses in that North Andover office, when I was questioning whether to abandon corporate security for island adventure, when I was selling stock footage while yearning for creative opportunity.

If I could advise that younger Alex now, I would say...well, let's make that my final chapter.

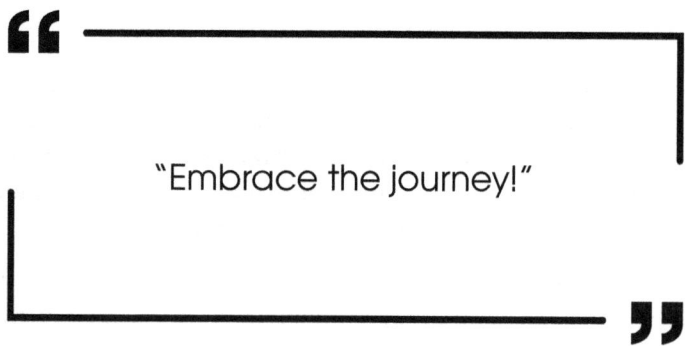
"Embrace the journey!"

# 21

# A LETTER TO MY SON

*Hey buddy,*

*As I write this, you're still too young to understand what I'm about to tell you. But someday, when you're figuring out your own path in this world, I hope these words might help guide you. I've learned a lot of lessons the hard way over the years, and if I can save you from making some of my mistakes—or at least help you see them coming—then this whole crazy journey will have been worth it.*

*When I think about the best advice I've ever gotten, one thing stands out. It came from Jerry Smith when I was just starting out at PineRidge: "Never get the big head." Just five words, but they've stuck with me through everything—when I won the Amazing Race, when my food show became the biggest thing on PBS, when our travel show took off around the world, when The College Tour grew into something I never saw coming.*

## Don't Let Success Go to Your Head

*Son, the world I work in—Hollywood—is full of stories about talented people who crashed and burned the second they got a little success. You'll see this everywhere, not just in entertainment. The writer who becomes impossible after one hit. The actor who starts treating everyone like garbage. The producer who stops listening to anyone once their show gets picked up.*

*It's never about talent. These people had skills. What they lost was humility. They got the "big head" Jerry warned me about.*

*Staying grounded will be hard work for you, too. Our whole world is set up to make you think you're special—all the attention on the people in front while ignoring everyone who actually makes things happen, the celebrity worship, the constant need to promote yourself.*

But here's what I want you to know: staying humble isn't just about being a good person. It's smart. The people who last? They stay curious enough to keep learning, they share credit, and they treat the intern the same way they treat the CEO.

This really hit me when we were trying to sell Around the World for Free. Network after network said no. We could've gotten bitter and defensive. "They just don't get it!" Instead, we listened. We took their feedback and used it to improve our idea. That humility when facing rejection? It led to something way cooler than what we'd originally pitched.

### Being Likable Will Be Your Superpower

The second thing I want to tell you: being genuinely likable is like having a secret weapon. Not fake charm—real likability that comes from actually caring about people, being reliable, and taking real interest in what others are doing.

Think about it, son. People hire, promote, and recommend people they actually like. You might be the most talented person in the room, but if you're a pain to work with? Good luck.

I learned this when I sold calendars door-to-door to pay for Brazil (yes, that story I've told you a hundred times). Success wasn't about being slick—it was about connecting with people, even for just five minutes on their doorstep. I'd ask questions, actually listen, and find something in common before I even mentioned the calendars. That same approach worked everywhere after that.

The key is being real about it. Genuine likability comes from actually caring about other people, appreciating different viewpoints, doing what you say you'll do, and wanting everyone to win instead of just looking out for yourself.

### Forget the "Master Plan"

Here's something else that might surprise you: I don't have some big end goal in mind. And I never have.

I know that goes against everything you'll be taught. Pick your destination, map the route, measure your progress. But honestly, buddy? The journey is the whole point.

Instead of chasing specific targets, I've focused on directions—connecting with people across differences, building things that open up possibilities instead of shutting them down, creating stuff that entertains while maybe changing how people see things.

Take the series Around the World for Free. *Burton, Zsolt, and I had this vision of an interactive travel thing. But we weren't married to the details—we cared about the core stuff: real cultural experiences, genuine human connection, letting viewers be part of the adventure. When networks said no to our original pitch, we didn't throw it away. We kept going...kept fighting, and eventually landed a deal with CBS (the largest network in the world at the time). I found that partnering with CBS resulted in something significantly better than we'd initially imagined.*

Same with The College Tour. *It started as me trying to help your cousin Isabelle with her college search. She could only afford one trip to look at schools, which seemed totally unfair. Now it's a huge thing that reaches millions of people. That growth wasn't part of some master plan—it happened because we stayed focused on trying to help solve a problem.*

## When Personal Problems Become Big Ideas

*Sometimes the best ideas come from your biggest frustrations. It was early 2020, and I was sitting in our garage talking to Burton, and the whole entertainment world just stopped because of COVID. I'd just finished some good projects, but suddenly everything felt uncertain. Your mom and I were planning to start a family (that would be you!), and I'm trying to figure out what's next.*

*That's when I told Burton about Isabelle's college nightmare—how she was stuck visiting just a few schools when she really needed to see what was out there. The unfairness was crazy: some families could afford to tour dozens of campuses while others were making life-changing decisions based on websites.*

*"Dude, that's brilliant," Burton said right away. Bring the college to the student instead of the other way around. Level the playing field.*

*The format made sense from all my production experience. Instead of the typical campus tour with one guide whose personality might completely color your view, we'd feature ten different current students sharing their real stories. You'd get the full picture of each school—the culture, academics, social life—that no single person could give you.*

*What happened next was one of those rare moments when everything clicks. Four of us—Burton, Lisa, Mike, and me—came together believing in this thing. "Let's not worry about money right now," Lisa and Mike said. "Let's just make this because we believe in it."*

*This wasn't some calculated business move. We all knew The College Tour would solve a real problem for millions of students and families. Unlike most TV projects that start with market research, this came from actual experience and wanting to fix something unfair.*

### What It All Means

*Now we're about to film our sixteenth season. We've done hundreds of schools—big state universities, tiny liberal arts colleges, Historicaslly Black Colleges and Universities, and technical programs. Millions of people watch across all kinds of platforms, and it's actually changing how students find and evaluate colleges.*

*But you know what makes me proudest? It's the messages from students who found programs they'd never heard of that turned out to be perfect. International students who got insights they couldn't get anywhere else. First-generation college kids who saw themselves in the stories we tell.*

*One message got to me, from a student in rural Alabama: "I always thought college was for other people—people with more money, better grades, different backgrounds. But watching real students who look like me, from places like my hometown, facing similar challenges... it made me believe I could belong there too. I applied to three schools I discovered through your show."*

*That's what makes all the crazy schedules worth it, son. We're not just making TV—we're opening up possibilities for students who might have limited their dreams because of money, location, or just not knowing what was out there.*

*What makes this so satisfying is how it brings together everything from this weird career path your old man has had. The storytelling I learned at PineRidge. The innovations from* Around the World for Free. *The production skills from Steve Harvey. Even the people skills from selling calendars. All these random experiences came together to make The College Tour possible.*

*Here's what I want you to remember: lasting success comes from three things working together—being good at something, staying humble enough to keep learning, and being someone others actually want to work with. You'll need all three. Without skills, opportunities don't turn into wins. Without humility, early success often leads nowhere. Without likability, doors don't open in the first place.*

Jerry's advice captured something important about making it in any field. Success comes from team effort, not individual genius. Growing means staying open to learning no matter how far you've come. The best opportunities come through real relationships, not slick self-promotion.

Your world will keep changing—new technology, shifting economics, and different cultures. Skills that seem essential today might be automated tomorrow. Business models that feel cutting-edge now might look ancient in a few years. But human connection? That stays constant. Being humble enough to keep learning will always make you adaptable. Being genuinely likable will always create opportunities. And combining those with solid skills will always work, no matter how things evolve.

These principles have guided my path from the little town of Georgetown, Massachusetts, to Brazil, to Germany, to the island of St. John, to racing around the world to hundreds of college campuses. Through all these different chapters, they've created steady growth despite setbacks, continuous learning despite changing circumstances, and real relationships across all kinds of situations.

And maybe most importantly, they're values worth living by regardless of what happens professionally—ways of being that create positive impact, whether you're making global TV or having a family dinner, building international business or volunteering locally, working on big creative projects or just navigating everyday life.

So when people ask me about my end goal—where I'm heading, what I'm trying to achieve, what legacy I want—my answer stays the same: I don't have an end goal. Never have. And that approach has led to something way more extraordinary than any destination I could have planned.

I hope when you're old enough to really understand this letter, you'll take these lessons and make them your own. The world will be different by then, but these fundamentals—humility, genuine connection, and embracing the journey—they'll still matter.

Love you, Mac.

—Dad